ETF | Exchange-Traded Fund | p. 174 ?

Free websites: – Yahoo Finance
– MSN Money

20 FOR 20: THE 8-STEP BEGINNER'S GUIDE TO VALUE INVESTING

THE 20 BEST STOCKS & ETFS TO BUY AND HOLD FOR THE NEXT 20 YEARS TO MAKE CONSISTENT PROFITS EVEN IN A BEAR MARKET

FREEMAN PUBLICATIONS

D1612174

HOW TO GET THE MOST OUT OF THIS BOOK

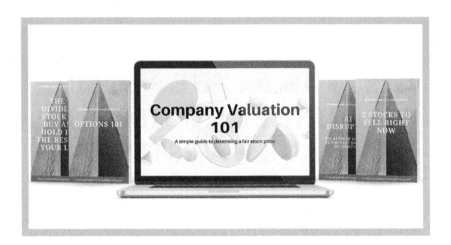

To help you along your investing journey, we've created a free bonus companion course that includes spreadsheets, bonus video content, and additional resources that will help you get the best possible results. We highly recommend you sign up now to get the most out of this book. You can do that by going to the link below

https://freemanpublications.com/bonus

Free bonus #1: Company Valuation 101 video course ($97 value)

In this 8 part video course, you'll discover our process for accurately valuing a company. This will help you determine if a stock is overvalued, correctly valued, or a bargain. Giving you an indicator of whether to buy or not.

Free bonus #2: Guru Portfolios Analyzed ($37 value)

In these videos, we analyze the stock portfolios of Billionaire investors like Warren Buffett. As well as top entrepreneurs like Bill Gates.

Free bonus #3: 2 Stocks to Sell Right Now ($17 value)

These 2 stocks are in danger of plummeting in the next 12 months. They're both popular with retail investors, and one is even in the top 5 most held stocks on Robinhood. Believe us; you don't want to be holding these going into 2021 and beyond.

Free bonus #4: AI Disruptor - The $4 Stock Poised to be the Next Big Thing in Computing ($17 value)

This under the radar company, which less than 1% of investors have heard of, is at the forefront of a breakthrough technology that will change our lives as we know them. Soon this technology will be in every smartphone, tablet and laptop on the planet.

Free bonus #5: Options 101 ($17 Value)

Options don't have to be risky. In fact, they were invented to *reduce* risk. It's no wonder that smart investors like Warren Buffett regularly use options to supplement their long-term portfolio. In this quick start guide, we show you how options work and why they are tools to be utilized rather than feared.

Free bonus #6: The 1 Dividend Stock to Buy and Hold for the Rest of Your Life ($17 Value)

Dividends are the lifeblood of any income investor, and this stock is a cornerstone of any dividend strategy. A true dividend aristocrat with consistent payouts for over 50 years which you'll want to add to your portfolio for sure.

All of these bonuses are 100% free, with no strings attached. You don't need to enter any details except your email address.

To get your bonuses go to

https://freemanpublications.com/bonus

CONTENTS

© **Copyright Freeman Publications 2020 - All rights reserved.**

The content contained within this book may not be reproduced, duplicated or transmitted without direct written permission from the author or the publisher.

Under no circumstances will any blame or legal responsibility be held against the publisher, or author, for any damages, reparation, or monetary loss due to the information contained within this book, either directly or indirectly.

Legal Notice:

This book is copyright protected. It is only for personal use. You cannot amend, distribute, sell, use, quote or paraphrase any part, or the content within this book, without the consent of the author or publisher.

Disclaimer Notice:

The following work is presented for informational purposes only. None of the information herein constitutes an offer to sell or buy any security or investment vehicle, nor does it constitute an investment recommendation of a legal, tax, accounting or investment recommendation by Freeman Publications, its employees or paid contributors. The information is presented without regard for individual investment preferences or risk parameters and is general, non-tailored, non-specific information.

Freeman Publications, including all employees and paid contributors, agree not to trade in any security they write about for a minimum of three days (72 hours) following publication of a new article, book, report or email. Except for existing orders that were in place before submission (any such orders will also always be disclosed inside the document). This includes equity, options, debt, or other instruments directly related to that security, stock, or company. The author may have indirect positions in some companies mentioned due to holdings in mutual funds, ETFs, Closed End Funds or other similar vehicles, and there is no guarantee that the author is aware of the individual portfolios of any of those funds at any given time. Such indirect holdings will generally not be disclosed.

Warning: There is no magic formula to getting rich, in the financial markets or otherwise. Investing often involves high risks and you can lose a lot of money. Success in investment vehicles with the best prospects for price appreciation can only be achieved through proper and rigorous research and analysis. Please do not invest with money you cannot afford to lose. The opinions in this content are just that, opinions of the authors. We are a publishing company and the opinions, comments, stories, reports, advertisements and articles we publish are for informational and educational purposes only; nothing herein should be considered personalized investment advice. Before you make any investment, check with your investment professional (advisor). We urge our readers to review the financial statements and prospectus of any company they are interested in. We are not responsible for any damages or losses arising from the use of any information herein. Past performance is not a guarantee of future results.

This work is based on SEC filings, current events, interviews, corporate press releases, and what we've learned as financial journalists. It may contain errors and you shouldn't make any investment decision based solely on what you read here. It is your money and your responsibility.

Freeman Publications Ltd. are 100% independent in that we are not affiliated with any security, investment vehicle, bank or brokerage house.

All registered trademarks are the property of their respective owners.

"I think it's a tragedy that the small investor has been convinced by the media that they don't have a chance. That the big institutions, with all their computers, all their degrees and all their money, have all the edges. And it just isn't true at all.

When people get brainwashed by the media, they act accordingly. They buy stocks for a week, then they buy options. They buy the Chile fund this week, and the Argentina fund the next week. Then they get results proportionate to that kind of investing, and that's very bothersome.

But if someone can sit back, and form their own opinion about a company or an industry, I think the public can do extremely well in the stock market on their own."

Peter Lynch, NYTimes Bestselling Author and one of the most successful investors in history. As manager of the The Magellan Fund he doubled the return of the S&P500.

STOCK INVESTING: A 30,000 FEET VIEW

What runs through your mind when someone mentions the stock market? Do you immediately think of a complicated machine that has the potential to bankrupt you? Alternatively, do you think of a place where you can double or triple your money in a matter of months?

Despite what you may hear from uneducated voices, the reality isn't close to either of these extremes. The stock market is a great place to build long-term wealth, but only if you make the right investment choices.

Between 1991 and 2020, the S&P 500, the index containing the 500 largest public companies in the US, returned an average of 9.77% per year.

But those who invested in individual stocks didn't fare as well. A study by Bernstein Advisors found that in the same time period, the average retail investor buying individual stocks made a return of just 2.1% per year. This means during the 30 year period, the "man on the street" underperformed every single asset class, including cash (as 3-month treasury bills).

So why does this happen? Why do so many individuals make below-average returns?

Much of it involves education or lack of it. When people are first exposed to the idea of stock investing, it's often presented as an excellent opportunity to make quick money. This is why, for many investors, their first experience is a bad one. A tip from a friend or family member entices them. Or worse, they see a post on social media about a "once-in-a-lifetime buying opportunity" and don't want to miss out on potential profits. You may have had this same experience in the past. If not, you likely know someone who has.

You may also have been lured by the prospect of making quick money by day trading stocks. Day trading is to investing; what visiting a casino is to starting your own business. Sure, you *could* win big at the casino, but you're very unlikely to, and over the long run, you'll go broke. This isn't just our own opinion. It comes from Etoro, one of the largest stock trading platforms in the world. Etoro discovered that 80% of their day trader customers lost money over their first year.

The financial media doesn't do you any favors, though. All of the reporting concerning the market is breathless. It's a land of extremes. Things are either going great, and you see superlative headlines such as "This is the stock market's best single day performance ever on a rainy Thursday in September."

Or alternatively, the headlines give the impression that things are falling apart without any hope in sight. Charts upon charts are displayed, and it seems as if every day brings news of some economic indicator causing turmoil in the markets. While the next day, everything is fine and dandy. One day it's the unemployment rate. Another day it's the manufacturing output. The third day it's automotive sales. Whatever it is, there is never a middle ground. Instead, there are always intense reactions one way or another.

In the past ten years, we've seen another force dominate the investing landscape, social media. Many new investors take to social media to get an understanding of where they should place their money. Not only is this the worst decision you could make (and we'll explain why later on in this book), it's a decision that often leaves you feeling burned and deters you from making future investments.

With these combined factors, it seems incomprehensible how a regular investor could ever be successful in the stock market. This leads many to seek professional advice. However, this search comes with its own set of problems. A 2013 study by the Financial Planning Association found that 46% of financial planners did not even have a retirement plan of their own. These are people licensed to advise others on sound financial decisions, yet they can't even get their own house in order.

Additionally, the term financial planner or financial advisor is somewhat misleading. These are not impartial third parties. Many people are not aware that a financial planner is primarily a sales role. For example, many advisors often recommend whatever funds pay the advisor the highest commissions when you buy them. Like any profession, there are, of course, great financial advisors who genuinely have the best interests of their clients at heart, but to ignore the other side would be naïve.

So if mainstream media isn't helpful, and professionals often have their own best interests at heart. Where do you start?

Even with an abundance of information at your fingertips, it is surprisingly hard to find basic information about investing. Much of this it is designed to be intentionally overwhelming so that you feel as if you *must* put your money in the hands of the so-called professionals.

Which is why our goal with this book is simple. First, we will dispel the common investing myths you see every day. Second, we'll show you how you can mute the noise around you and only focus on what matters. Third, help you develop your own repeatable and reliable process for analyzing which companies to buy and when to buy them.

Investing is not a get rich quick scheme. Our answer to the question "what's the best way to make $1 million in the stock market quickly" has always been "start with $2 million".

There are rare occasions where you will make fast returns. For example, our email subscribers who acted on our recommendation of personal tailoring company Stitch Fix captured a 140.24% return in just 99 days. That being said, the majority of your profits will come in 5-10 years, not 5-10 weeks.

Investing is not gambling. We've seen an alarming trend of new investors treating the market like a casino with high risk strategies like buying leveraged options or day trading, and we aim to reverse that trend.

This is not a book about technical analysis (or, as we like to call it, technical astrology). We adhere to great investors like Warren Buffett, Peter Lynch, Carl Icahn, and Charlie Munger. People who have made consistent returns in the market over the long haul by focusing on the companies behind the stock, not charts or formulas.

In a world of instant gratification, we focus on the simple things. On identifying well-run businesses that serve a need for a significant market. Companies that have a competitive advantage and are whose stocks are available at a fair price. We'll explain more about these principles further in Chapter 4 where we outline our selection process.

For now, we thank you for purchasing this book. As Warren Buffett would say, the best investment you can make is an investment in yourself, and by buying this book, you've done just that.

"THERE ARE 2 RULES OF SUCCESSFUL STOCK INVESTING:
RULE NO. 1: NEVER LOSE MONEY.
RULE NO. 2: NEVER FORGET RULE NO. 1."

- Warren Buffett

WHY INVEST IN STOCKS IN THE FIRST PLACE?

A question that is often at the forefront of a new investor's mind is: Why should I even invest in the stock market? There seem to be so many other opportunities to make your money work for you, such as real estate, buying precious metals, and even cryptocurrency.

It turns out that the latest generation of adult Americans is the least invested one when it comes to the stock market (Martin, 2018). A CNBC survey indicated that only 23% of millennials preferred investing in the stock market compared to other options.

The reasons for this are understandable. Since 1995, the financial markets have witnessed near-constant turmoil every five to ten years. First, there was the dotcom bubble, which wiped out many inexperienced investors. Then markets were thrown into chaos by 9/11. We then experienced a period of enormous growth that culminated with the housing crisis between 2007-2009. After that, we had a decade long bull run to record highs, which ended at the beginning of 2020. At the time of writing, the markets have mostly recovered. But thanks to the lingering effects of the Covid-19 crisis, we are still in an uncertain period.

Despite this perceived instability, the stock market is not something to be avoided. The numbers are simple. Over 50 years between 1966 and 2015, the S&P 500 returned an annual rate of 9.69%. In real terms, this means you would have made 102 times your initial investment after 50 years. If those same returns hold over the next 50 years, a modest investment of $5,000 today will be worth $510,000 in 2070. These numbers assume you don't make *any* additional investments during that time, which is unrealistic, and with additional investments, your eventual return will be far higher.

This book will show you how fluctuations and market dips are not things to be feared. The strategy we recommend will help you not only ride out those dips but even thrive when turmoil strikes the markets.

How can we do this? It's straightforward. Many people fail at investing in stocks because they think about stocks in fundamentally flawed ways.

Investing in stocks is simple. This doesn't mean it's easy, but you don't need an advanced degree in calculus or statistics to make consistent long term profits.

We're here to tell you that the way the markets work is far more straightforward, and you don't need a high IQ, a specialized degree, or any secret code to 'unlock' them. Your stocks will provide you with profits as long as you're willing to do the work and can think about them correctly.

Where Investors Have Gone Wrong in the Past

Consider how the average novice investor behaves in the market when they first get started. This person has some extra cash on hand. They've heard that investing is a good idea because just holding onto the cash will make them a victim of inflation. The days of getting a decent interest rate on a savings account are long gone. In fact, Wells Fargo's *Way2Save* account pays just 0.01% interest.

So a novice investor's first step is to head over to a financial adviser for stock recommendations. The other option, which we see more in 2020, is posting in a Facebook Group asking for tips on investing $500/$1,000/$10,000. This is the first mistake novice investors make.

They then sink their money into a random assortment of companies, primarily based on tips from strangers or a carnival barker on TV. Then sit back, hoping for vast sums of money in return. After all, when everyone on social media posts about how much their stocks are going up, it seems like a sure thing.

It seems like a game when they switch on CNBC, or open their Robinhood app to check on their newly held companies. They see red and green signs moving up or down, a horizontal bar at the bottom with symbols moving right-to-left, another bar below it that moves a little slower, pundits exhorting secret strategies and killer stocks to buy.

After a while, the novice investor sees their stocks either take a dip or they don't grow as fast as expected. So they become impatient. Their stock is down 20%, and they are not happy. So they decide to sell because the guy on TV is now telling them to buy another "hot new issue" instead. They don't completely understand the logic behind this, but do it regardless. Soon the stock they sold begins to rise, and they rush to buy in again, only this time a higher price than what they previously sold at.

They successfully buy when prices are high, and sell when they're low, which is the opposite of the most basic tenet of investing.

Some investors go even further and decide to try their hand at short-term moves like day trading or buying options. A few manage to do this successfully, but they are the extreme exception, not the rule. Any kind of financial trading has a significant survivorship bias. You only hear about the success stories. But for every success story, you aren't hearing about the ten people who failed in the same endeavor. The fact of the matter is, depending on the source, 80-99% of day traders lose money in the long run. This is why we won't be discussing day trading or any other short-term financial strategy in this book.

What to do Instead –Rational Process Investing

You're going to learn all about the correct thought process to adopt regarding the markets and how you need to analyze stocks. This book also contains 20 stocks that meet our buying and holding criteria for the next 20 years. All of these stocks fulfill the needs of our Rational Process Investing system, and you're going to learn exactly why this is.

For those of you tempted to just skip to that chapter, this is not a call to action to buy these stocks today because you'll also need to understand what is and isn't a fair price to pay for a stock. We'll be explaining that as well later on in the book.

In addition to all of this, you're also going to learn about asset allocation and diversification strategies. How you choose to invest your money directly impacts the return you can expect to earn in the markets. A thorough evaluation of your risk tolerance is necessary, and we'll show you exactly to do this.

Our combined investment experience over the years has placed us in the best position to help both new and experienced investors make the best decisions possible. You don't need to overcomplicate stock investing. Follow some sound principles, master your emotions, and you'll make more money than you'll ever need in the markets.

By understanding the concepts listed here and you'll be ahead of 95% of retail investors. Successful investing *does not* require you to have advanced degrees in math or statistics. In fact, there is little correlation between intelligence and successful investing. Even a genius like Sir Isaac Newton famously lost his entire Fortune (around $3m in today's money) in the South Sea Bubble of the 1700s. When asked about this, Newton was quoted as saying

"I could calculate the motions of the heavenly bodies, but not the madness of the people."

What you will need for success is some basic arithmetic (or access to MS Excel/Google Sheets), but more importantly: The ability to reason, the confidence to back your judgment, and the awareness to know when you are wrong.

First let's jump in and take a look at the very basics of successful, long-term stock market investing!

1

WHY THE LONG-TERM OUTLOOK?

W hat is the secret to successful investing? The answer will shock you. It is to do nothing. Well, not quite nothing, but our point is that to be successful, you need to limit your activity as much as possible when managing your investments. Tinkering with your portfolio every other day and second-guessing yourself is what causes more losses than any market dips.

This chapter will walk you through the investing philosophy known as "buy and hold" investing. You'll learn why this is far superior to any other investing approach for new investors.

THE DIFFERENCE BETWEEN SPECULATION AND INVESTMENT

Before understanding why buy and hold is such a powerful philosophy, we need to take a step back and understand the differences between investing and specu-lation. The first person who pondered this question was Benjamin Graham in his legendary book *The Intelligent Investor*. The book Warren Buffett frequently refers to as his "Bible."

According to Graham, investing or an investment operation was something based on what he called "intelligent principles." This ensured that it had a high probability of success. In contrast, speculation was carried out using unsound principles and had a high chance of failure.

This definition sounds simple enough, but there are many caveats here. What qualifies as intelligent, and what are unintelligent principles? In the context of stocks, we can define an intelligent investment process as one that takes the market's financial realities into account.

The first reality to acknowledge about stocks is that **no one can predict stock prices in the short term**. This is because, in the short term, stock prices are fueled by emotion. These emotions arise from the myriad of psychological biases that human beings have.

For example, you hear about everyone jumping into a hot new stock and see the media telling you that this company is a sure thing. You're likely going to think that this stock is great. This herd mentality or peer pressure is just one example of unconscious biases we carry. Since Graham's time (during the Great Depression), this behavior has been a factor and it is still present today.

FREEMAN INVESTING RULE #1

IN THE SHORT-TERM, PRICES ARE FUELED BY EMOTION
IN THE LONG-TERM, PRICES ARE FUELED BY MATH

To further illustrate how flawed behavior affects the markets in the short term, let's discuss "Flash Crashes." A flash crash is a market crash (defined as any drop of 10% or more) that occurs over the span of a few minutes or even seconds. Flash crashes have become more common these days thanks to the advent of algorithmic trading, a method of automatic trading based on pre-determined variables.

Two "Flash crash" incidents occurred in the past decade. These incidents perfectly illustrate the short term drivers of the market and the irrational nature of human behavior. The first occurred on August 24th 2015. The minute the markets opened, they immediately fell by 5% before gaining back most of their gains by the end of the day. The Grandaddy of all flash crashes occurred on May 6th, 2010 when a single trade caused the entire market to lose 1,000 points (roughly 9% of its total value) and then rise right back up in under 15 minutes.

Many stocks reached unthinkably low prices. Accenture, the global consulting conglomerate, actually saw its stock touch zero before rising back up to $41.09. Similar massive movements occurred in the crash of 2015 as well. All of these movements led to much hand wringing in the media.

The talking heads put forward complex reasons for why the crash happened. The widely accepted explanation for the 2015 crash was that traders were nervous after the previous session on a Friday. The market had declined, and they weren't sure what was going to happen over the weekend. The Chinese markets, which open before the American ones, opened lower, and hence this fueled a rush of selling in America.

Let's just take a step back from all of this madness. If the market was to be believed, a 54 billion dollar company at the time, such as Accenture, was temporarily deemed as being worth nothing because a bunch of Chinese traders happened to sell their stocks in China. Furthermore, the market then decided that the same company was worth 54 billion dollars by the end of the day.

Does any of this sound logical? Let's say you own a piece of farmland that is consistently producing high-quality crops. A person comes up to you and declares that your land is now worth zero. He goes away and then returns eight hours later and tells you that your land is now worth $1 million. You'd rightly think that this person is a nut!

Yet when the stock market does the same thing, we invent intelligent-sounding drivel such as "traders were nervous over the weekend, and Chinese selling triggered a wave of sell orders on the open."

We can learn from cases like this that the markets are *incredibly irrational* over the short term. Therefore tailoring your actions to these short-term moves will only result in you being exposed to this madness. So what is the best approach to adopt?

Short Term Trading Versus Long Term Investing

Short term trading involves all kinds of risks because of moves such as these. In essence, a trader is attempting to gauge how the market feels about the stock. Here's an experiment for you to conduct. Walk over to your partner and try to guess how they're feeling about something. You might be able to guess what is wrong some of the time, but not all the time. Now walk over to a stranger and try to imagine how they feel about something. You don't know this person, but your task is to guess anyway. How often do you think you'll succeed? Finally, try to imagine what some random person on the other side of the planet feels about Walmart's stock price. You don't know anything about this person or what their motivations are. All you know is that they have an opinion about the price of Walmart stock.

You'd come back saying that this is a hopeless task. How could you possibly know any of this? Well, this is what traders try to do every day. They seek to take advantage of short term price moves, and as you've already seen, these moves often don't occur thanks to logic or business reality. They occur due to emotion. This can be as simple as a large financial institution placing a big order to sell the stock, so everyone else starts selling as well. What we see here is an example of the herd mentality in action.

It stands to reason that if you wish to take advantage of these moves, you need to predict the emotions other traders have concerning the stock. It is impossible to do this in real life, but traders think that using indicators and angled lines on a chart will somehow solve the issue for them. Does this sound like an intelligent thing to do? Welcome to the world of speculation!

Speculation isn't restricted to merely trading. It is anything you carry out in an unintelligent manner, and this encompasses many things. For example, your third cousin Vinny calls you up, telling you about this excellent opportunity to invest in a tanning salon. Vinny says this is a "sure thing," and you could double your money in the next six months. If you were to go ahead and put your money in the salon without doing your due diligence, this would be speculation, not investing.

Given that stock market prices are driven by emotion in the short term and that we cannot predict emotions, it stands to reason that we need to take a longer-term view of the market. There is an excellent reason to do this because emotions tend to exhaust themselves over the long run. As Benjamin Graham said, the market is a voting machine in the short term, but it's a weighing machine in the long term.

Think about your own life and set the markets aside for a second. How often have you seethed in anger for a few minutes and then forgotten all about it a week, a month, or a year later? Do you remember if you lost your temper this time last year? We're not talking about situations where the emotion was justi-fied thanks to life events. We're talking about those issues that seem petty in the long run. Your spouse or partner placed their shoes over yours and dirtied them, and you lost your temper. The dog decided to pee all over your new carpet and so on. The delivery driver was 10 minutes late because he got lost. What would have happened if you had followed that emotion's lead and made huge changes in your life? Would this have been the smart thing to do?

Of course not! Instead, you gave yourself time to calm down, and when you did, you forgot all about it and moved on. The same thing works in the market as well. On August 24th, 2015, the actions of Chinese traders were extremely crucial. Yesterday, Amazon stock couldn't care less about what Chinese traders did. It's all emotional.

Over the long run in the market, a company's stock price reflects its underlying earnings growth. Using the example of farmland that you own, the land's real value is the crop yield it produces. It also depends on how profitable farming is as a business. Are you getting good prices for your crops? If so, the land is quite valuable if it produces high-quality crops. If not, it isn't as valuable.

The same applies to companies. New investors often miss one key element: **There are real companies behind those little symbols you see on the screen**.

Buying shares is the same as owning a percentage of the company. These are businesses with suppliers, customers, competitors, and employees. All of these factors come together to generate profit and loss. The more profit they make, the more prosperous the company is, which is reflected in the stock's price over the long term.

While you cannot predict human emotion, you can make intelligent decisions about a company's business prospects. You can evaluate their economic outlook and that of the business they're operating in. This process removes emotion and market sentiment from the equation and is the only way you can reliably make money in the long-term.

Understanding the Costs of Investing

Now that you understand why having a long term view is essential, it's time to look at costs. Investing in stocks is not free. You will need to pay your broker (or these days, a website or app) commissions when buying or selling stocks.

After all, it can be off-putting when you want to invest $100 but then discover you need to pay $10 in commissions to buy a stock. Fortunately, this isn't a big deal these days because there are a ton of reputable brokers who offer very low and even zero commission accounts. We'll be talking about our personal favorite later on in this book.

While commissions are less of an issue than they used to be, taxes haven't changed. As it relates to the stock market, you will pay taxes on capital gains and dividends. Dividends are distributions from the company to you, and as such, they represent passive income.

You don't have to pay anything other than the price of a share to earn a dividend. As such, paying taxes on them isn't too painful since they effectively reduce your investment cost. We want to add that companies are not obliged to pay dividends, and not all do.

Capital gains taxes operate differently. Capital gains are the profits you make when you sell your investment. This is the difference between the sale price and the purchase price of your investment.

For example, if you buy one share of Disney at $100/share and then sell it once the price reaches $120, that $20 difference is your capital gain. Taxes on capital gains will reduce your overall profit. One area that can confuse new investors is when you actually must pay capital gains tax.

You only pay capital gains after you sell your investment. Therefore, the more you sell, the more taxes you pay. In turn, the more often you sell, the lower your overall gains are going to be.

Then there's the issue of long term versus short term capital gains taxes. The short term tax rate, which applies to investments that lasted less than a year, is the same as your income tax rate. In the United States, the long-term rate falls between zero and 20%.

Therefore, the longer you hold onto your investments, the less you pay in taxes. If you never sell your investments, you'll never pay capital gains taxes. In the real world, you will want to sell your stocks at some point since this is the only way you'll get to enjoy the fruits of your investment unless you want to pass them onto your next of kin in your will. Our point is that it is smart to avoid selling a stock within the first year of owning it.

Another cost you need to take into account when investing is inflation. Inflation is a hidden cost, and many investors fail to take notice of this. The value of a dollar tomorrow is not the same as a dollar today.

The best way to reduce the impact of inflation on your gains is by holding your investments for as long as possible, so they have the greatest chance to appreciate. We will explain more about taking inflation into account in our chapter on calculating a business's true value.

FREEMAN INVESTING RULE #2

REMEMBER TO ACCOUNT FOR INFLATION WHEN ANALYZING YOUR INVESTMENTS

It should come as no surprise to you that stocks rise at a far greater distance over the long run than they do in the short run. A good way to think about this is to ask yourself: Can you get more done in a minute or over a year? The answer is obvious. Hold onto your investments for as long as possible and give them a chance to make money.

By combining the above principles, it is clear that the most intelligent investment decision you can make is to buy and hold stocks for as long as possible. Leave the constant jumping in and out to the traders and other speculators. Resist everything that can potentially cause you to sell early.

So if you're planning to invest for the long term, this means you need to prepare well by researching your investments and then investing your money in the right way. You can then minimize taxes and transaction costs by holding for long periods. The longer you hold onto your investments, the longer they have to appreciate in value, which reduces the impact inflation has on your returns.

2

DEFINING YOUR INVESTING GOALS

A ll journeys need a goal. But getting just setting a goal is not enough. You'll need to plan how you'll get there. Our minds are like a GPS in that unless you specify where your destination is, you run the risk of wasting time going down the wrong path.

This chapter will help you figure out the goals you should have and the mindset necessary for succeeding in the stock market.

PREPARATION

Successful investment planning begins before you decide to invest in the stock market. Ensuring that you have a stable financial base before you invest in the market is essential since this will prevent you from making mistakes. For example, if you don't have the cash to pay your bills, you're going to be tempted to sell some of your stocks before they have a chance to blossom fully.

Figuring out where your investment capital will come from is crucial. Let's take a look at the kind of money you should be investing in the market

CAPITAL

At Freeman Publications, we adopt a long term approach. We apply the rule of thumb that all the money you invest in the stock market is money you will not need for at least ten years.

To prepare a sound financial base for yourself, we recommend that none of the following should be invested in the markets:

1. Your rainy day fund – 3-6 months' worth of living expenses that you've saved up in case you or your partner lose your jobs. The goal of your rainy day fund is that you never touch it. You should keep your rainy day fund in nothing riskier than a bank CD, and ideally, have at least one month's worth of expenses in physical cash.

2. Tuition payments - Money you needed to pay bills or your child's tuition should not be invested in the markets. If your children are younger, then, by all means, invest money you plan to use for tuition in the future, but have a ten year timeframe for your stocks to appreciate.

3. Down payments - Even if you're planning on purchasing a home in the next 2-3 years, don't rely on the stock market to generate enough money for a down payment.

FREEMAN INVESTING RULE #3

ONLY INVEST MONEY THAT YOU DON'T NEED FOR THE NEXT DECADE.

In short, do not rely on the market to make you money quickly, or generate money you need to pay your bills tomorrow.

This may seem like a pessimistic outlook, but in reality, it works very well. By not having to rely on your stocks for money, you remove the feeling you 'have' to make money. Many short-term traders and speculators get caught up in this emotion and end up making fatal mistakes that lose them money.

Here is a typical "I have to make money" scenario. A person places a stock trade, expecting a quick bump in price. The trade doesn't go their way, so they exit their position for a 10% loss. Losing money is tough to deal with mentally, and in their frustration, they open another position in a different stock. This trade goes against them as well, and they exit that position for another 10% loss.

Now their frustration turns to anger. So they place the third trade, this time for a bigger position than they usually would, in an attempt to recoup the losses from their first two. They tell themselves that this trade should go in their favor because the last two trades went against them.

Unfortunately for them, the market has no idea how their previous one, two, or 100 trades went, and the odds are no more in their favor than on trade number one. This third trade goes against them as well, and they cash out for another 10% loss.

This isn't a book about trading, but from this example, it's easy to see how the irrational nature of human beings cause short-term thinkers to lose money. If we extrapolate this behavior pattern over a more extended period, you can see why over 80% of day traders fail.

But no matter if you're a short-term trader or long-term investor. The markets are highly emotional, and you *will* be caught up in their whirlwind at some point, no matter how rational you think you are. Therefore, it is best to minimize your chances of doing something emotional in the first place. So when the time does come, you won't be at an emotional extreme that causes you to make poor choices.

The next step in your journey is to figure out your risk appetite.

Asset Classes and Risk

The concept of risk management is highly misunderstood in stock investing. When you speak to an average financial advisor, they'll explain risk to you in two ways. The first is to use your age as a barometer for it. A common rule of thumb is to subtract your age from 100. Then use the resulting number to measure what percentage of your money you should invest in stocks.

For example, if you're 40 years old, they'll tell you to place 60% of your money in stocks and 40% in bonds. This ratio is an oversimplification at best and plain wrong at worst.

The thought process behind this is that an older person needs to invest for income while a younger person should aim for price appreciation. If you follow this rule, though, every year, you will end up selling profitable stock investments and keep moving that money into new bond investments. The timeline for your bond investments keeps increasing while that of your stock investments keeps decreasing.

What if you find a profitable stock to invest in when you're 60 years old but have already allocated 40% of your money to stocks? Should you simply let this opportunity slip? This makes no sense. The real determinant of whether a person needs to invest for income or capital gains is their financial situation, not their age. 60-year-olds tend to have assets on hand, and if they have still have a secure income, why should they invest in bonds and fixed income?

The second manner in which people explain risk to investors is by using asset classes. You're told that small cap stocks (the shares of companies under $2 billion in size) are risky, and large cap ones are less risky. In turn, bonds are considered less risky than stocks and options. Once again, this is an oversimplified version of the truth.

The asset class of a stock does not indicate its risk. Let's say you were Jeff Bezos back in 1995. You have had a good career in finance and have money saved up. You get the idea to start this company, let's call it Amazon, and you have a clear vision of where you want it to go. You trust your abilities and know that you have the wherewithal to succeed.

However, your financial adviser tells you that starting Amazon (and by proxy, investing your money in it) is extremely risky. Mr. Bezos is 31 years old and should invest 69% of his money in stocks, with 60% of them in large cap stocks, 5% in mid caps, and the rest in small caps. Amazon is a startup and is none of those. Let's say Bezos loses his mind momentarily and decides to follow this advice.

Given that he's worth approximately 124 billion dollars today, largely thanks to his Amazon ownership stake, it's safe to say that this would have been a hall of fame worthy mistake to make.

FREEMAN INVESTING RULE #4

RISK IS DEFINED NOT BY THE ASSET CLASS OF YOUR INVESTMENT, BUT BY YOUR EXPERTISE IN EVALUATING IT

The same factors apply when analyzing small-cap companies (defined as a company with a market capitalization of less than $2 Billion) versus large-cap companies. The commonly held belief is that small-cap companies are riskier than large-cap companies.

This might be true in a general sense, but it is not correct on an individual level. If you know a small-cap company inside and out, it is a far better company to invest in than a large cap like ExxonMobil or Goldman Sachs, where even the CEOs likely don't have a full clue as to where the company's money is going.

If you're unsure about the extent of your expertise, it's best to outsource it to capable managers who know what they're doing. A financial adviser or your broker is not a capable manager. Instead, investing in index funds and ETFs is the way to go.

Index funds and ETFs follow broad based indices in the market. By purchasing a single share of these funds, you can gain exposure to all of the fund's underlying stocks.

For example, one of the most popular ETFs is the SPDR S&P 500 Trust ETF, although you may know it by its ticker symbol SPY. SPY is a weighted index containing all 500 stocks in the S&P 500. The size of the stocks themselves weights the fund, so the largest stocks (Apple, Microsoft, Amazon and Google) make up a larger proportion of the fund than the smaller companies. Buying a single share of SPY gives you exposure to all 500 companies. By definition, owning SPY will always give you an average return each year because the S&P 500 *is* the average for US investors.

In addition to asset allocation, you need to evaluate your personal risk tolerance. Let's take a look at some of the factors that will help you define your risk tolerance.

Risk Factor #1 - Time

How much time do you wish to devote to the markets? The more time you can commit to analyzing companies and figuring out how they do business, the more risk you will be able to bear since you'll be able to spend more time mitigating it. This doesn't mean you need to be glued to the markets 24/7 like most traders are. For long-term investors, this behavior is counterproductive.

However, you will need to spend more time monitoring the companies you invest in if you wish to absorb more risk. You will need to spend more time finding quality companies to invest in, and you will need to spend time thinking about how to exit your investments correctly.

If you wish to make your investments passive, then you cannot have too much of your portfolio in single companies and will need to diversify your portfolio so that the risk is spread out. We'll be explaining more about proper diversification in chapter 5.

Risk Factor #2 - Your Expertise

Everyone is good at evaluating some form of business. You might not think of yourself as an expert or even a business person. But many businesses out there are straightforward to figure out. There is an equal number of complicated companies.

If you wish to invest in a complicated business, you'll need to evaluate it more. You might find that even after spending a lot of time, the company makes no sense to you, and you're unable to figure out its prospects. Therefore it's far better to choose simple companies to invest in, especially when you first start. You're going to have a better grasp of their economics, and you'll make better decisions as a result.

Just because a business is simple does not mean it can't make great returns. For example, in 2014, while trendy tech companies like Facebook, Netflix, and GoPro dominated the financial news cycle, the best performing stock on the S&P 500 was Southwest Airlines, which grew more than 110% in a single year.

As of December 2020, the best performing stock in the S&P 500 so far this year has been Etsy. Etsy is a very simple business. They're an e-commerce company that primarily sells handmade and vintage goods as well as craft supplies. Etsy stock is up 273% this year, because the number of people buying (up 55%) and selling (up 42%) on their website has increased significantly compared to 2019. More customers and more sellers mean more revenue, which means the company can justify a higher stock price.

Additionally, you have far more experience in your own company's sector than the average Wall Street analyst. This is why it's a good idea to begin with companies in the sector you know most about.

Even if you don't have much experience working in a sector, you are still a consumer. For example, let's say you're a coffee drinker, and you visit Starbucks every morning before work. If that location is always busy, it's a good indicator. If it's always empty, then it tells you the opposite story.

Let us be clear; understanding a company or using a company's products is not the *only* reason to invest in a company. It is crucial to make this distinction because many new investors use this as their <u>entire analysis</u> on whether a company is a good buy or not. But it is a great place to start your research.

To give you a real-life example of how being a consumer is a great place to begin your research. One of our best investments over the past decade has been McDonald's. Our research process started when one of our team commented that they'd traveled to over 30 different countries, and had never seen a McDonald's location that wasn't busy.

Risk Factor #3 – Emotional Risk Tolerance

Let's say you've invested a sum of money in the market. You promptly see that the stock has declined by 30%. What do you do? What are your emotions at that moment going to be like? Will you have the confidence and discipline to act rationally despite this huge dip?

People don't take the time to ask themselves if they're willing to lose more than half of their investment <u>on paper</u> before it ever makes them a single cent. Instead, everyone dreams of stock prices soaring and doubling their money in a matter of months.

This can and does happen occasionally. However, you cannot expect constant rises without experiencing dips. So the question you should ask yourself is, how much of a dip are you willing to stomach? Your investment in a single stock is far more likely to see a serious dip than the entire market will.

If the entire market, or an index fund that tracks the market, dips by a lot, you can rest assured that it will bounce back unless something truly catastrophic happens. It is unlikely that all of these companies will disappear overnight and for the markets to remain at zero forever. However, a single business can lose most of its value in a short time period.

Therefore, evaluate how much of a loss on paper you're willing to stomach, and adjust your investments accordingly. If you're only willing to accept a 15-20% loss on paper in your investment, then sticking to index funds and ETFs is your best choice. If you're going to invest in individual stocks, be prepared to stomach a loss of at least 30% on paper. On paper is the operative phrase here, because you don't realize a loss until you sell your stock.

FREEMAN INVESTING RULE #5

YOU MUST BE ABLE TO MENTALLY SEPARATE
PAPER LOSSES FROM REAL LOSSES.

INITIAL INVESTMENT AMOUNTS

The best way to begin investing in the market is via a tax-free retirement account. Maximize your contributions to it, and if your employer offers a 401(k) with matching benefits, make full use of that as well.

We typically advise people to invest at least $5,000 in the markets when starting. This means $5,000 in total investments, not $5,000 per company.

This is because to capture meaningful gains, your investment amount needs to be somewhat significant. Turning a $100 investment into $1 million is an unrealistic scenario. Turning $1,000 into $1 million is unlikely but still possible. Turning $10,000 into $1 million is completely achievable with the right company. With smart investments, turning $100,000 into $1 million is expected.

Those numbers might sound unrealistic, but you must remember the power of compound interest. With a 9.69% annual return rate (the market average) it takes 26 years for $100,000 to turn into $1 million. With a 15% rate of return, it only takes 17 years. With a 20% rate of return, it now only takes 13 years to reach your $1 million target.

The way to get compounding to work for you is to invest a large sum of money and be patient. Let's look at this via an example. Let's say there are two investors Anne and Bill. Anne invests $1,000 in the market and Bill invests $5,000. Both of them earn modest 7% gains over the course of 30 years. What is the value of their portfolios at the end of the 30 year period?

Anne's portfolio has grown to $7,612, while Bill's portfolio has grown to $38,061. The amount by which Bill's portfolio has grown is $33,061 which is far more than the paltry $6,612 that Anne witnessed. This is why it is essential to capture the power of compounding by investing a larger amount of money.

However, this doesn't mean that you should hoard your money until it reaches $1 million and only invest then. You need to give it time to grow as well. This is why we recommend a minimum amount of $5,000. From the above example, you can see that even this modest amount grows to quite a significant sum over 30 years.

If you don't have $5,000 but are determined to make a start, then go ahead. Providing you do proper research, investing in stocks is nearly always a superior option to just holding cash in a savings account. If you only have a small amount to invest, it's essential to choose the right investing platform because you don't want massive commissions to eat away at your potential profits.

How to Place Orders

If you already have a brokerage account, then you can go straight to chapter 3. However, if you do not, we've included a short guide for opening your first brokerage account.

With the rise in comparison websites, it can be overwhelming to choose an investing platform. We'll simplify the process for you. For new investors, there are 3 major factors which matter most when selecting a platform to use.

1. The commission structure (how much you have to pay each time you buy or sell a stock)

2. What financial instruments you can buy (stocks/bonds/ETFs/mutual funds)
3. How user-friendly the platform is

Based on the factors above, we recommend the Robinhood platform for new investors in the United States. The most significant selling point of Robinhood is that it is commission-free for buying and selling common stocks. Zero commission is important because if you *are* only investing small amounts, fixed commissions on each buy or sell order can put a significant dent into your potential profits.

You can read our complete guide to setting up a Robinhood account by using the link below.

https://freemanpublications.com/how-to-buy-stocks-online

More experienced investors will likely favor other platforms like E*Trade, TD Ameritrade or Charles Schwab. Each of them have their pros and cons, so we advise you to do your research and pick the one best suited to your situation.

For readers outside the US, a simple Google search for "Best investing platform in [your country]" will let you compare your options. But here are some low-cost platforms that our readers have personally recommended from their own country.

- UK – Freetrade
- Canada - Wealthsimple
- India – Zerodha
- Brazil – XP
- Most EU countries - DeGiro

3

THE 7 BENEFITS OF LONG TERM INVESTING

There are many benefits to following the buy and hold strategy, and this chapter will go in-depth and explain what these are. You've already learned about a few of these in the first chapter. You'll now gain a better understanding of them.

TAX ADVANTAGES

We've already mentioned the tax portion of your investment consideration. By investing for longer periods, you'll significantly lower your capital gains tax bill. Currently, here are how taxes on long term capital gains (gains on investments held for more than one year) are assessed in the United States.

- 0% capital gains:
- Single filers earning up to $40,000
- Married joint filers earning up to $80,000
- Heads of Households earning up to $53,600
- Married separate filers earning up to $40,000
- 15% capital gains:
- Single filers earning from $40,001 to $441,450

- Married joint filers earning from $80,001 to $496,600
- Heads of Households earning from $53,601 to 469.050
- Married separate filers earning from $40,0001 to $248,300
- 20% capital gains:
- Single filers earning above $441,451
- Married joint filers earning above $496,601
- Heads of Households earning above $469,051
- Married separate filers earning above $248,301

As mentioned earlier, short term tax rates are assessed based on your current income levels. This means you'll always be paying higher taxes on your short term investments than on your long term holdings.

We can see the true impact of paying short term capital gains taxes when we think terms of compounding. From the previous chapter, you've already seen that a $10,000 investment growing at 7% every year matures to $76,122 after 30 years. Let's say you pay 15% taxes on this amount. Your final take home amount after tax is worth $64,703.

Let's say you invested $10,000 every year in a one-year investment and that this investment gained 7% as well. Since this is a one-year investment, you'll sell it and pay a tax rate of 25% on the gains before reinvesting the after-tax amount the following year. How much does this investment mature after 30 years?

It grows to $46,415. That's $18,288 less than if you had just held the entire time. In other words, if you had avoided withdrawing your money and paying higher taxes on it at the end of every year, you could have earned close to 40% more money. That's a pretty significant difference!

MORE EMOTIONAL DISCIPLINE

We always counsel readers to invest their money with the mindset that they will not need it for ten years at the very least. This doesn't mean that you need to hold onto your investment for that long, but it helps put the importance of your investment in perspective.

If you knew prior to making an investment that you will need to hold onto this stock for ten years, you're far more likely to do your homework and follow rational principles. Think of it as buying a piece of furniture or renting an apartment for the next ten years. Would you rush in and move without taking a good look at the place? Would you neglect to carry out due diligence? Unlikely.

Another reason why buy and hold works very well is that, contrary to popular perception, most investors do a decent enough job of figuring out which stocks they want to buy. It is the selling that they find tough. You need to sell your investment to realize gains and once your stock has amassed a good amount of unrealized gains, your challenge begins.

Let's say your investment has risen by 25% over a year, which is a phenomenal return. The following year, the market begins to decline, and your investment is now displaying an unrealized gain of 10%. Your brain immediately thinks that you've lost 15% gains when in reality, all of this is on paper. You haven't lost anything.

The financial media often reports of market declines as 'wiping out' a certain amount of money. They also make statements such as 'investors lost $1 trillion.' These are nonsensical statements. You will lose or make money only when you sell your investment. Buying and holding removes the pressure of figuring out when to sell since you need to hold onto it for as long as possible.

We'll address the issue of selling shortly.

PASSIVE INCOME

We've already mentioned the existence of dividends as they relate to stock investment. Dividends highlight why the traditional approach of risk, in terms of income investment in bonds versus capital investment in stocks, is flawed. You can invest in stocks and still earn a good income.

Dividends allow you to earn income from your stocks, regardless of whether the stock price goes up or down. Dividend yields on stocks generally hover between two to five percent. It is possible to earn higher yields, but you need to take certain factors into account.

A stock's dividend yield is calculated by dividing the dividend payment amount by the stock's price. The higher the payment is, the higher the yield is. However, the price plays a role as well. A declining stock price can also push yields higher, so it's not as if chasing yields is the best way to spot great dividend-paying stocks.

It's a bit like earning rent on a property you've bought. The best part is that you're not going to have to pay to maintain your stock investment, unlike the rental property. You don't need to chase tenants for payments; you don't need to conduct regular maintenance, you don't need to advertise for tenants and so on. You simply invest your money, and you get paid a dividend.

Finding this level of passivity in any investment outside the stock market is impossible. What's more, the longer you hold onto your investment, the more income you earn until your effective cost of investment decreases. For example, if you've paid $200 for stock and are receiving two percent yields annually, you're earning $4 as income on your investment. Once you receive the first payment, you've made a realized gain of $4, and therefore your effective cost is now $196.

The longer you hold, the lesser the effective price is, and you'll increase the odds of you making a profit.

ENTRY PRICE DOESN'T MATTER (AS MUCH)

Short term traders worry a lot about getting the exact prices they want on entry. This is because if you're going to buy at $95 and sell at $96, entering at $95.50 will make a huge difference. You'll reduce your potential gains by 50%.

When investing over the long term, though, your exact entry price doesn't matter. After all, your investment horizon is at least ten years long. A dollar here or there over ten years will not matter if you invest in a great company with long-term prospects.

In other words, if you identify a company primed to move upwards, it is going to move by a big distance over the next decade. What will it matter if you entered at $95.50 instead of $95 in such a scenario?

LONG TERM INVESTING IS LESS STRESSFUL

Buying and holding is far, far easier than trying to actively trade your money. We've already mentioned the futility of timing the market. Or trying to predict the emotions present in the market. With buy and hold, you identify a stock that you like, do your homework on it, buy it, and that's it, you're done.

You receive huge tax advantages and free up your time to find even more great stocks to invest in. By removing the headache of trying to figure out when to exit, you'll also sleep better. Take it from us!

NO NEED TO CHASE UNICORNS

A unicorn is that magical stock that has the potential to increase in value by 10,000%+ in a short timeframe. Many venture capital investors chase this sort of thing, and it is a tough thing to do. Most of the time, venture capital investments fail due to the extremely high risk involved. We see a similar venture capital mindset with people who choose to only invest in penny stocks.

With buy and hold, you'll remove the need to chase these extraordinary gains because your mindset will shift.

You'll realize a good investment that earns 10-12% every year, even if it is before taxes, has serious power when it comes to building wealth. Over the long term, this sort of investment is what makes money, instead of finding that magical stock that increases 100 or 1,000 fold in a short period of time.

The best way to find these unicorns is to practice a long term holding strategy. This way, you give your investments enough runway to grow instead of expecting them to increase by this amount over the course of one or two years.

FREEMAN INVESTING RULE #6

LONG-TERM
INVESTING HAS MULTIPLE ADVANTAGES
OVER SHORT-TERM TRADING

YOU CAN PRACTICE PROPER DIVERSIFICATION

Diversification is another term that gets misconstrued by new investors. The reason for diversifying is that it helps reduce volatility and risk in your portfolio.

For example, if you had your entire portfolio in Apple stock and a sudden supply chain issue meant the company couldn't manufacture any iPhones for 2 years, you would be in trouble.

But if Apple were one of the many companies you owned, the drop in Apple stock price would not have as big of an effect on your overall returns.

Now the problem we see with short term investors is that their diversification strategy falls into the category of "Diworsification," a term coined by Peter Lynch is his 1989 classic *One Up on Wall Street*

Before we cover proper diversification, we will outline the two most common "Diworsification" strategies new investors have.

Diworsification problem #1: New investors often overexpose themselves to a single industry, which increases their risk without maximizing the upside.

47

We see this frequently with trendy sectors (like marijuana) or people looking for perceived bargains during market downturns (like airlines). They load up their portfolio with every large and mid-cap company in the sector, hoping for a quick buck, but are left holding the bag when the entire industry hits a downturn or doesn't recover as expected.

FREEMAN INVESTING RULE #7

JUST BECAUSE YOU OWN A LOT OF DIFFERENT COMPANIES DOES NOT MEAN YOU ARE DIVERSIFIED.

Diworsification problem #2: New investors get so caught up with the idea of owning stocks that they think *everything* is worth buying. They easily justify this decision by telling themselves that they are becoming more diversified with each additional company they own. Before they know it, they own more than a hundred different companies with tiny positions in each one. Unless you're doing this full time, there is no way you can keep up with the inner financial workings of 100+ companies in a variety of sectors.

On top of this, diversification is not proportional. By that, we mean each new company you own does not provide an equal amount of diversification. In their book *Modern Portfolio Theory and Investment Analysis*, Edwin Elton and Martin Gruber showed that by owning 20 stocks, your portfolio risk was reduced by an average of 29.2%, when compared to just owning 1. But by owning 1000 stocks, your risk was only reduced by a further 0.8% when compared to owning 20.

There is no magic number for how many stocks you should own, but for a novice investor, we think the sweet spot is between 10 and 30. We chose 20 companies to profile in this book because we believe 20 to be a good number of companies for an individual investor to hold at once. It's enough to have exposure to a broad range of industries (which you can supplement further with sector or index-tracking ETFs), but a manageable number meaning you can keep track of each company's performance.

Now that we've covered seven advantages of long term investing, let's get into the meat of it and examine the factors you should look for when finding a great company to invest in.

"IF YOU KNOW WHAT YOU WANT AND WHY YOU WANT IT AND WHEN YOU WANT IT, YOU'LL GENERALLY PAY A LOT LESS FOR IT THAN YOU WILL IF YOU BUY SOMETHING THAT SOMEBODY ELSE PERSUADES YOU TO BUY"

- *Gerald Loeb*

4

RATIONAL PROCESS INVESTING

So far, we've discussed the importance of doing your due diligence on the stocks you plan on investing in. In this chapter, we'll introduce you to our process of analyzing a stock's prospects. For long-term investments, we like our stocks to meet specific criteria that give them an advantage in the marketplace today and fuel their growth for years to come.

THE WARREN BUFFETT TEST

The Warren Buffett test isn't a single criterion. The aim here is to follow the simple principles that Buffett talks about when he mentions his investment criteria. A regular statement he has often made is that he looks for companies run by great management teams.

This means that he values integrity and honesty in them, aside from competence. Adherence to expanding the company's bottom line and giving shareholders the highest possible return for their investment needs to be their top priority (LaRoche, 2019). While he does aim to buy entire businesses, he's thrilled to own a percentage of a good business as well.

This is because a profitable business is one of the best assets a person can own. A company that is regularly expanding its bottom-line earnings and is growing them at a certain rate like clockwork is hard to find. Therefore, selling it doesn't make sense. Your aim should be the same.

These kinds of companies do not sell for cheap, however. The market is aware of how good they are, and as a result, you're unlikely to find the stock selling for a 60% discount from its value. Buffett focuses on finding great companies and paying a fair price for them instead of finding average companies at great prices.

The average company will have to be sold since its earnings are unlikely to grow forever (which makes it average after all). This means Buffett needs to find better investments and keep searching constantly. By buying a great business, he gets to work once and earn profits forever. This doesn't mean he never sells. It's just that his mindset upon entry is to ask whether he wants to hold onto the business forever.

By doing this, he automatically screens for great companies, not mediocre ones.

UNDERSTANDING THE BUSINESS

We talked about briefly in chapter 3 regarding buying stocks in business whose products you consume. This is a great starting point for your research, but you need to *truly* understand the business, before you invest in it.

If you decide to buy Walmart stock, make sure you understand the ins and outs of Walmart's business. Can you explain what Walmart does in 30 words or less? Alternatively, could you explain your rationale to a 10 year-old so that he/she would understand? If not, you probably don't understand it well enough.

For example, you might think you know all about a movie streaming company's operations (like Netflix) simply because you have a Netflix account. But if you don't know basic numbers like how many new subscribers they are adding per quarter or what percentage of their revenue they need to reinvest into content creation, you shouldn't buy shares until you know these numbers. The good news is, they're easier to find than you think.

We are not saying Netflix is a good or bad investment at this time. But our point is that many Netflix investors don't understand how the company works, and more importantly, where it plans to make its money or the challenges it faces in the next 5-10 years.

It's also important to distinguish between the surface level business the company is in, and their bottom line profits. For example, McDonald's might be a "fast food company," but the real money is made in its real estate business and franchise model. The fast food business is just a catalyst for this. While ensuring that food gets made quickly and on time is a priority, this is not what really drives the company's profits.

McDonald's owns the real estate on which all its restaurants are built. The company then turns around and leases them to its franchisees and charges them rent that is well above market price. They can do this because of McDonald's brand strength, meaning franchisees are willing to pay a premium on rent. One estimate placed rental costs at 22% of gross profits per year from a franchisee's perspective (Daszkowski, 2019). This gives the company a significant cushion to weather tough business conditions.

Even if sales do decline, the company still owns all of its locations, and it doesn't have to worry about tenants not paying rent. It can repurpose its sites with ease and create new revenue streams. This is a significant advantage in the fast food business.

Another example of a business that is seemingly in another line of business is Starbucks. The company is a coffee chain on the surface, but really, it's in the third space business. What Starbucks is selling is not coffee. Instead, it's a place you can spend time that isn't your home or office. It is where people meet one another for informal meetings, catch up, and go on dates. It is a convenient place to work from as well, given the rising number of remote workers. Sure, the coffee prices are higher than immediate competitors like Dunkin Donuts, and this is something that detractors point out over and over. However, people still opt for Starbucks over cheaper alternatives, and it is not a detriment to the business. Many Starbucks naysayers will laugh at the idea of paying $5 for a cup of coffee, but if their customer base thought this way, they would have gone bankrupt in the 1980s.

Differentiating between sector and company

A common problem with new investors is they buy into the hype of shiny new industries. In the past few years, we've seen Marijuana, sports betting, biotech, 5G, and other "hot sectors" have their days in the sun and become the 'cool' industries to invest your money. In 2020, the two hottest sectors were electric vehicles and pharmaceuticals (because of the COVID vaccine race). It's not uncommon to meet a new investor with more than 50% of their portfolio in one of these sectors.

In the image on the next page, you'll see a visual representation of how most investors think about new industries. They only take first order consequences into account. These are the most apparent consequences of a catalyst event.

The catalyst event example we've used in the image is the legalization of medical marijuana in the United States, which began on a widespread basis in 2016. The first order consequence is the most obvious move. In this case, this was that because of the new laws, demand for marijuana would skyrocket. This led to novice investors buying up every marijuana company they could get their hands on. However, many investors never move their thought process past the first order consequences.

An investor focused on second order consequences would have been thinking about oversupply or the difficulty that many marijuana companies had securing land leases. They then would have discovered a company like Innovative Industrial Properties, which leases land and offers financing to marijuana growers. IIPR has grown its share price (excuse the pun) 800% in the past three years, while marijuana growers themselves have suffered. The lesson here is that if you can identify the second and third order consequences of any catalyst event, then you have a better chance of finding undervalued companies with huge potential.

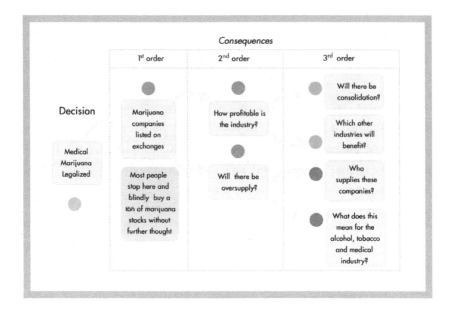

It's essential to make a distinction between sector growth and company growth. Just because 5G will be a prominent sector in the next 5-10 years does not mean *every company* with 5G exposure will be a good investment.

A growing sector is a good place to start your research, but it's not a good place to end it.

As we've said previously, the best place for you to start is the sector or industry you work in. Even if the 5G or Marijuana industries appear sexier than the industry you work in, you probably don't understand them nearly as well.

CEO/FOUNDER IS STILL RUNNING THE SHOW

Many companies that have their founders still in place as the CEO tend to be safer investments because founders understand their businesses a lot better than outside CEOs do.

This directly translates into results for investors. A study by Purdue University found that S&P 500 companies who still had their founder in a significant role, outperformed companies without the founder involved by 310% over the past 15 years.

The example of technology companies is a good case in point. Almost all of them are run by their founders, and they operate in extremely competitive environments. While Apple has been an exception, Microsoft's fate is an excellent example of how the lack of a founder at the helm leaves a company vulnerable in a changing and dynamic industry. When Bill Gates stepped down in 2000 to focus on his charity work, the stock traded sideways for the next 16 years until Satya Nadella revitalized the company by pivoting its focus to the cloud computing industry.

Even Apple would not have grown to its current size without the leadership of Steve Jobs. In the years when he was ousted (before his return), the company's fate provides a good example of the dangers of externally hired CEOs running the company.

INTANGIBLE ASSETS

Also known as "what you won't find on the balance sheet". A company has two types of assets: Tangible and intangible. A building or a factory is a tangible asset, as are the goods that the company produces. Intangible assets are a bit trickier to nail down. For example, Coca-Cola has one of the most significant intangible assets in the world: Its trademark.

The phrase "Coca-Cola" is recognizable all around the world. If we were to pour Coca-Cola into another bottle and call it "Freeman Cola," would you drink it? Even if it tastes the same as Coca-Cola, you'll be unlikely to switch your preference to the new drink. This is the power of an intangible asset.

Ferrari is another company that has a similar pull. Swap the badge on a Ferrari with anything else, and people will suddenly want to pay far less for it, even if it is in the right shade of scarlet. The best companies have some form of intangible assets that work for them. This could be a brand name, a patent, or a process that gives them a competitive advantage in the marketplace.

Management quality is also a critical intangible asset. For example, Apple under Steve Jobs had one of the biggest intangible assets that could not be quantified on their financial statement. Their asset was Jobs himself. Disney is another example of a company with significant intangible assets in intellectual property and multiple generations of globally recognized characters.

MANAGEMENT QUALITY

It isn't easy to evaluate the quality of management. Most shareholders look at the stock price and then reverse engineer whether management is any good. This is a bit like looking at the quality of windows in a house and figuring out whether it's a good investment. There's a lot more to it than just that!

One of the biggest qualities you need to look for in management is its ability to adapt. For example, Kodak was one of the biggest companies in the photography space, thanks to its development of the film. When the digital revolution came, it doubled down on film and is now just an afterthought.

The development of the smartphone, in turn, left many digital camera producing companies in the dust. Some pivoted successfully to making high-end cameras for professionals (Canon, GoPro) while others never quite made the leap (Vivitar). It often comes down to honesty.

Honesty in communications is one half of this. How willing is management to disclose the business conditions to shareholders in their reports? Are they willing to admit faults and mistakes? Do they frankly discuss the upcoming head-winds for the business? Another part of honesty is management's ability to stop themselves from drinking their own Kool-Aid.

The Management's Discussion and Analysis (MD&A) section of the company's financial reports provides a good read on how honest management is. Reading prior reports and looking at how management evaluated the business environment is a good way to get a handle on how they tend to communicate and view conditions. An excellent example of this was Jeff Bezos' letters to shareholders when Amazon was still a fledgling company. Bezos constantly reiterated his vision for the business and did not focus on minutia, like whether they hit a Wall Street analyst's earnings estimates. This is the kind of long-term thinking you want to see from management.

We saw a similar situation with Mark Zuckerberg's actions around 2012. Zuckerberg gets a lot of flack, but an undeniable fact is that he knows his business inside and out. Following the iPhone's release and the rise in mobile use, Facebook remained buried in the desktop era and risked obsolescence. He didn't mince words when he announced that Facebook needed to switch to focus on the mobile experience because otherwise, it was facing extinction (Wagner, 2019). His foray into getting a Facebook phone manufactured failed, but his other efforts paid off, and Facebook is now firmly established as a giant.

On the flip side, we have examples of CEOs believing their own hype. While it wasn't a public company, the saga of Theranos' Elizabeth Holmes is instructive. While she has a large list of faults, almost all of her conduct stems from the fact that she could not be honest with herself about what the company could deliver in a reasonable timeline.

A recent public example is that of Trevor Milton at Nikola. Nikola was one of the electric vehicle success stories of 2020, seeing its stock rise more than 750% in just five weeks and being valued at more than $30 Billion. However, there were serious concerns about the battery technology that Milton claimed would revolutionize the industry. Instead of addressing concerns, Milton doubled down on his assertion that Nikola had the best tech out of any of its peers. However, there was a major problem. The technology didn't exist. This wasn't the only thing that didn't exist. Milton even embellished insignificant details, such as the number of solar panels on the corporate headquarters. This pattern of lies led to Milton resigning as CEO in September 2020 after the SEC announced it would be investigating him for securities fraud. Nikola stock has since plummeted 80%.

STRONG SALES AND MARKETING OPERATIONS

These divisions of the company are the lifeblood of the organizations. Not all of us might like salespeople, but their efforts go a long way towards ensuring the company makes a profit. The organization of a company's marketing efforts provides useful insight into how careful the management is when deciding on the company's future.

Consider that Facebook still runs ads for itself, and Google still publishes direct mail pamphlets to get businesses to advertise with them. These efforts show that the management is not complacent despite occupying a premier position in their industries.

Coca-Cola is another example of this. They have one of the most substantial intangible assets globally, yet they feel the need to advertise themselves. Looking at the turnover and quality of managers in charge of sales and marketing is an excellent way to gauge how much the company values this part of the business.

One crucial element of this principle is knowing which numbers matter the most to a company's bottom line. For example, many Software-as-a-Service businesses have many free users (who cost the business money in server fees). Still, they have a difficult time converting these free users into paying customers.

So when reading a company's annual or quarterly report, focus on figures such as **paying** customers or average customer purchase value. Rather than relying on misleading numbers like "total users" or "monthly average users." Unprofitable companies often use these to make their prospects look more attractive than they are.

LONG TERM FOCUS

You're investing for the long term and therefore, you want to invest in companies that align with that focus. It isn't easy running a public corporation. There is constant media pressure and analysts' opinions shifting the focus from long term health to short term profits.

A typical scenario that often occurs with companies is this. The CEO decides to allocate capital towards a project that will ensure long term competitiveness. Doing this requires significant cash and increases the company's short term debt burden. This has the effects of reducing earnings during that quarter.

Wall Street immediately reacts and begins questioning the company's motives. Will the long term project really work? Will they be able to sustain the short term earnings projections? Earnings projections are figments of analysts' imaginations that they expect companies to adhere to. If the company doesn't meet this standard, a wave of selling begins, and the stock price gets depressed.

This, in turn, enrages shareholders who begin to think that the analysts were right after all. A good manager knows how to manage both sides of the equation. Short term projections need to be hit, but long term projects need to be prioritized.

Bill Gates was a good example of this back when he ran Microsoft in the 1990s. The company always magically hit analysts' projections and still managed to drive competitors like Apple out of the market at that time. It isn't an easy job, but that's why the CEO gets paid what they do. Someone obsessed with short term prospects and worried about the damage it will cause their reputation is unlikely to produce long term growth at the company.

DOES THE COMPANY HAVE AN ECONOMIC MOAT?

This is a term Warren Buffett uses frequently when speaking about things he looks for in a potential investment. Internally, when one of our team brings up a new company to research, our first question is often, "where's the moat?".

An economic moat is some condition that gives a company a significant competitive advantage. It could be anything from size to trademarks and patents or a business process.

For example, Amazon's size offers it a considerable economic moat. The company offers customers bargain-basement level prices, and it's able to do this thanks to its sheer size. Its average cost per unit is far lower than what a smaller retailer can offer, and thus, Amazon can afford to earn a small percentage of profit, but it sells so much of it that the amount of profit it earns is high.

Coca-Cola has a strong economic moat through its brand name. Everyone recognizes it, and everyone buys it because of that. Interestingly, both Amazon and Coca-Cola are owned by Berkshire Hathaway, Buffett's investment vehicle.

Another factor that can create a moat is a large number of users. For example, Google and Facebook are popular thanks to the large number of users they have. This is an example of a moat caused by the network effect. This happens when companies build a significant userbase. This userbase provides a better customer experience, which fuels growth leading to an even higher userbase.

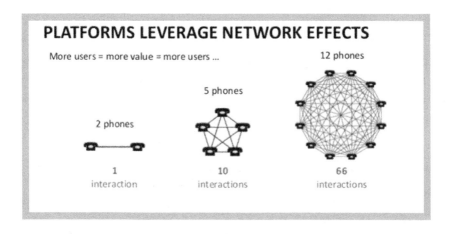

Facebook is a perfect example of this. There comes a tipping point in many people's lives where not being on Facebook is more detrimental to their quality of life than on it. Take for example, a woman in her early 60s. For a long time, she considered herself technophobic and avoided social media as a result. However, she has just become a grandmother for the first time, and her daughter has explained that the best way to get pictures of her new grandson is to use Facebook. She then realizes many of her friends are on the platform, so she encourages her other friends who don't yet use the platform to sign-up. All of this creates a better user experience for the people on the platform and fuels more growth. We see similar examples in the workspace communication space with companies like Slack and Zoom.

Other examples of moats are companies operating in non-sexy industries. Non-sexy industries are great because companies receive less analyst attention, they are less prone to disruption, and the incumbents can often have a natural monopoly.

A great example of this is Waste Management. You don't have to be a genius to figure out which industry the company is in. Now imagine being an employee of Waste Management. If you met someone at a BBQ, would you introduce yourself as your job title "I work in marketing," or would you let them know you work for a company called Waste Management. Besides, there aren't too many 20somethings in Silicon Valley spending all night on caffeine and Adderall hypothesizing on how to disrupt the waste management industry. That is a big reason why the stock is up 400% in the past decade.

Another factor that can cause a moat is a company operating in a morally or ethically dubious industry. Tobacco, alcohol, and casino companies all fall under this category. We should note that you should never compromise your moral or ethical views just to make money. The beauty of long term investing is that you can eliminate pretty much any industry you *don't* want to invest in but still make a killing in sectors that do fit within your views or beliefs

One trap new investors fall into is mistaking pioneering for a moat. What we mean is this: people assume that being first gives a company a significant competitive advantage. This really isn't true. Does anyone remember Altavista or Orkut? You may have never heard of those names. Altavista was a popular search engine that existed before Yahoo search did (remember when Yahoo, not Google was the search king?) As for Orkut, this might shock you, but Google was one of the first companies to build a social media platform, and it was years ahead of Facebook. However, the site was shut down in 2014 after it lost market share to other platforms.

You might point to Amazon as a counter-example of this, but even Jeff Bezos' company was not a pioneer. Book Stacks Unlimited came a full three years before Amazon's original avatar of an online bookseller. Our point is that pioneers are the ones that deal with all the obstacles and inefficiencies only for the newcomers to take advantage of processes that have been built. This results in them growing faster and eventually obliterating the pioneer.

CAN THE COMPANY WEATHER A STORM?

How robust is a company's business model? Can it withstand a stress test? Stress tests are scenarios where analysts project profitability numbers based on the assumption of adverse conditions. For example, a hotel chain is unlikely to survive an 80% vacancy rate for too long before things get ugly. Airlines are also notorious for their inability to handle the slightest disruption to their business conditions.

For every business, a standard stress test is a reduction in sales. The higher the business's ability to withstand this stress, the safer your investment will be. Another example of a stress test is multiple Acts of God in quick succession for the insurance industry.

This is why recessions destroy companies built solely on debt, whereas companies who maintain healthy cash reserves (like Berkshire Hathaway) can ride the wave through to the other side.

Another essential element of this principle is that a company's income is not reliant on a single factor. For example, if a semiconductor manufacturer relies on a contract with Apple for 80% of its revenue, then Apple ending that contract would plunge the economics of that business into disarray. This is exactly what happened with the UK firm Imagination Technologies. It had a deal with Apple to provide graphics processors for the iPhone. This single contract accounted for 45 percent of the company's total revenue. After Apple ended the agreement, the stock took a huge hit and was down 71% from its peak.

As we explained in the previous chapter as to why diversification is essential as an investor, the same applies to the businesses you invest in. Don't buy companies that are overexposed to a single economic factor.

FREEMAN INVESTING RULE #8

WHEN ANALYZING A BUSINESS, REMEMBER TO TAKE INTO ACCOUNT THE POTENTIAL DOWNSIDE RISK.

"WHEN MOST INVESTORS, INCLUDING THE PROS, ALL AGREE ON SOMETHING, THEY'RE USUALLY WRONG."

- Carl Icahn

5

WHAT DOESN'T MATTER WHEN ANALYZING STOCKS

T here are many misconceptions about what matters when researching companies to invest in. In this chapter, you're going to learn about some of the most popular ones. A lot of this advice is peddled in the mainstream, and you might be surprised to hear that much of it is incorrect. Keep an open mind throughout this chapter and evaluate the arguments we make for yourself.

DIVIDENDS

Dividends are a good thing to have in stocks, and we do not deny that. However, there is investing literature out there that elevates dividends to a God-like status. Dividend investors claim that the presence of a dividend alone justifies investment because it signifies that the stock has a ton of advantages within it.

Chief among these is the argument that dividends ensure that management will not act recklessly since they know that they have to pay the dividend. This makes them take fewer risks and thereby guarantee a safe and steady income stream. Let's start with this claim and look at some of the purported advantages to see whether they make sense.

Dividends Ensure Stability

The presence of a dividend does ensure stability but only to a point. The fact is that managers routinely maintain dividend payments for fear of adverse effects on the stock price. Some investors believe this is a good thing because it forces management to look after shareholder interests. This kind of thinking happens because investors are unable to evaluate the quality of a company's management effectively.

FREEMAN INVESTING RULE #9

THE PRESENCE OF A DIVIDEND IS NOT AN ADEQUATE SUBSTITUTE FOR A THOROUGH EVALUATION OF THE QUALITY OF MANAGEMENT.

Poor management is perfectly capable of paying a dividend and still running a company into the ground. Let's say poor management takes over a company and carries out some less than promising projects. Revenues decline, but management knows that stock prices will remain steady as long as they can maintain the dividend. This is because many investors favor dividends far too much.

However, since revenues are declining, the dividend represents a greater portion of the company's earnings. As this proportion (called payout ratio) increases, there's less money available to allocate to projects to ensure the company maintains its competitiveness.

In short, the dividend causes management to stop looking at the future and start focusing on the present instead. This is the exact opposite of what proper management does. Notice that the presence of the dividend cuts both ways. In the presence of good management, it is a good thing, but it can turn into a disadvantage when poor management is in charge.

Therefore, the dividend, by itself, means nothing. Using it as a barometer to measure stability is incorrect. A business is a multi-faceted entity, and reducing the question of stability to a single factor is wrong. Don't misunderstand this point to mean that poor management will always pay out a greater proportion of earnings than good management.

It all comes down to the nature of the business. Some businesses don't require much reinvestment, and therefore, a 90% payout ratio might make sense. This is the case with Real Estate Investment Trusts (REITs). Some businesses require significant reinvestment, and in such cases, paying even 10% is a considerable feat and is an indicator of excellent management.

Another argument posits that stable companies in stable industries pay dividends. This is true to an extent. However, it ignores the fact that an unstable sector does not necessarily mean that the companies are bad investments. If you had a chance to invest in Google back in 2004, would you take that chance today? What about Amazon in 2001 or Facebook in 2014?

None of these companies pay a dividend, and they probably never will. This doesn't mean they're bad investments or that they're unstable. As an example, Berkshire Hathaway has never paid a dividend since Warren Buffett bought it in 1964. He purchased the company for $11.50 per share. The current stock price is $340,000 per share. It's safe to say his investors are quite happy with his performance.

Dividends Represent Shareholder-Friendly Managers

The term "shareholder friendly" has been turned and twisted to mean a lot of different things. These days the very presence of a dividend gives management an automatic "shareholder friendly" label. From the scenario presented in the previous example of poor management maintaining the dividend, is this really a shareholder-friendly thing to do?

Surely, the better thing to do would be to suspend the dividend and absorb the short term blowback. As long as the long term investment plays out, who cares what the stock price will do in the short term. Shareholders who value the business and understand the long-term consequences of the decision will find this a lot friendlier than those that insist on investing based on a few media tropes.

Dividends Over Capital Gains

A particularly problematic attitude that accompanies dividend investing is that dividends matter more than the capital gains a stock provides. Here's the thing that many dividend lovers miss: Capital gains will always be a more substantial portion of your investment return than dividend payments will be. The average dividend payment represents between 2-3% percent of the stock's price.

A rise of even 4% per year in the stock price means that capital gains outstrip dividend gains. Where do capital gains come from in the long term? From earnings, of course. This is also where dividends come from, or stable ones at the very least. The lesson here is that you need to pay attention to the stock's earnings prospects and not just its dividends.

TRENDY COMPANIES

This is a common pitfall that many investors walk right into. They read the news and feel that they have to be a part of the industry of the future. Alternatively, they think that some company has been in the news quite a lot recently and therefore, it must be a good investment.

Many companies manage to attract shareholders by being media darlings. A great example of this is Enron. The energy firm was once the golden child of Wall Street, and named "America's Most Innovative Company" for six years straight. In 2001, Enron declared the largest bankruptcy in history, after it was revealed that systematic accounting fraud had plagued the company for years. In just 18 months, the share price went from $90 to zero.

FREEMAN INVESTING RULE #10

DON'T INVEST IN THE HYPE. EXAMINE THE
UNDERLYING BUSINESS AND INDUSTRY
PROSPECTS INSTEAD.

CONSENSUS OPINION

There is no shortage of opinions when it comes to stock analysis. We're not talking about the casual gossip that occurs between you and those around you. Professionals indulge in gossip-mongering as well. The difference is that they get paid to do it.

Wall Street analyst opinions hold great sway over the short term movement of the stock's price. A sell rating or a downgrade (which is when an analyst becomes less bullish on a company's prospects) can cause the price to move down in a hurry, while a strong recommendation can create hype that pushes its price up equally quickly. This happens because large numbers of people hang onto these analyst ratings as a crutch and use them as a substitute for conducting stock analysis themselves.

However, examining the relationship between analysts, the trading desk of an investment bank, and the companies they analyze is instructive. A good case that highlights this relationship is that of Amazon back in 1997. This was the year that Amazon filed its IPO.

Filing an IPO is not an easy task, thanks to the large number of regulatory hurdles that exchanges and the authorities impose. Companies have to hire an investment bank to ensure the process is carried out smoothly. Often, investment banks prepare years in advance in anticipation of a possible IPO. It was no different with Amazon.

The company was a darling of Wall Street thanks to Jeff Bezos' efforts and analysts regularly touted its strong balance sheet and earnings prospects. The primary driver behind such reports was the fact that the number of users on the internet was set to explode, and this put Amazon in prime position (once again, excuse the pun) to capture their shopping activity.

There was just one problem. The company wasn't making any money. Amazon famously pushed everything back into its businesses to achieve size, and for many years, its free cash flow was dangerously low. None of this mattered to analysts, however. Asking whether Amazon could ride out such low levels of cash with constant venture capital injections was a reasonable thing to do.

Yet, no one did this. A big reason for this was that Wall Street was actively courting Amazon in anticipation of its IPO. Morgan Stanley was the firm that ultimately won the contract, in no small part due to its analyst Mary Meeker's glowing reports of the company. Although Meeker denied that the business she generated for Morgan Stanley had anything to do with her ratings (Schwartz, 2000).

In contrast, the lone analyst that questioned Amazon's business policy found himself pushed aside by his firm Lehman Brothers. IPOs are enormously profitable for investment banks since they earn money in two ways: The first is via fees, and the second is through trading profits. The stock that is initially sold to the public comes directly from the promoter or investment bank. Naturally, the aim here is to sell it for as much as possible since this results in the highest profit. Given that analyst opinions count for so much, it stands to reason that the analysts at the bank would talk up the stock.

However, Wall Street insists that a so-called "Chinese wall" exists between the analyst and trading departments. The track record and ethics of this industry is a matter of public record.

The point here isn't about whether analysts were right or wrong. In this case, Meeker was right about Amazon in the long run. However, it certainly wasn't due to the reasons she cited in her original glowing reports. Amazon almost went bankrupt during the dot com crash around the turn of the millennium.

The thing for you to note is that analysts' opinions and the market consensus aren't worth the paper they are printed on. There are many conflicts of interest inherent in the process, and the story of Amazon's IPO and the role analysts played in it is instructive. Amazon fixed its issues, and despite this, the company was unloved in the mid 2000s. This was a case of analysts being wrong once again by holding onto outdated opinions.

While Amazon is an example of how things eventually worked out and how problems were brushed under the carpet, the credit crisis of 2007-2008 is an example of when all these issues were laid bare. In that case, it wasn't just analysts' opinions that were the issue, but the same system was at work.

Analysts at rating agencies rated complex derivatives as "investment worthy" primarily because Wall Street banks would not approach them for business unless these ratings were provided. This caused sophisticated investors to invest in them, and the result was a complete meltdown (Lewis, 2011).

So, the next time you hear the chatter on TV or social media saying that stock X is due for a rise or that stock Y is scheduled for a fall, take it with a truckload of salt. There are other factors at play here. Acting based on hearsay is an example of groupthink. You're better off following the simple analytical framework that we've already highlighted.

MARKET SENTIMENT

Closely related to groupthink is the phenomenon of market sentiment. Is the market going up or down? Popularly peddled financial wisdom often states that you should not try to time the market. But how the media covers financial markets causes investors to do this exact thing.

Who cares what market sentiment is at the moment? Remember that in the short term, prices are driven by emotions and not logic. By focusing on investing for the long term, you're going to place yourself in the best position to ignore all the chatter that will cause you to sell low and buy high.

A great piece of advice on this comes from legendary investor Peter Lynch. We should note that this quote is from 1994, but you can reliably substitute newspapers for online news or social media.

"If you own auto stocks, then you shouldn't be reading the financial part of the newspaper. Instead, read the section of your local paper about automobiles. See how they talk about new car models, which ones have good reviews, and which ones stink. That is what you should be reading. You shouldn't be checking stock prices four times a day. Checking stock prices first thing in the morning is not useful. You shouldn't be dealing with the minutia of "what's the market doing today". Instead, focus on "what is this company going to be doing two years, three years, five years from now."

— PETER LYNCH

NUMBERS IN ISOLATION

There is no single number on a balance sheet or financial statement that tells a company's entire story. For example, Price to Earnings ratio (PE) is often touted as a good indicator of the fair value of a company. But PE differs drastically between sectors. For example, healthcare services have an average PE ratio of 42, which is almost 3x the entire market average. So if you only decided to invest in companies with a PE of 20 or less, you'd miss on great companies in the healthcare services sector.

The same goes for something like earnings growth. If a company is up 20% in the past year, that could be incredible. Or it could be worrying if all their competitors are growing at 100% during the same period.

With any financial numbers, you need context. This is why it's essential to analyze a company's competitors during your research phase.

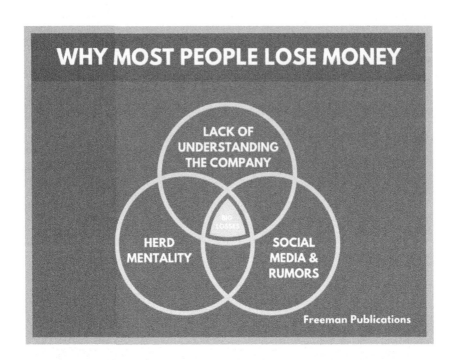

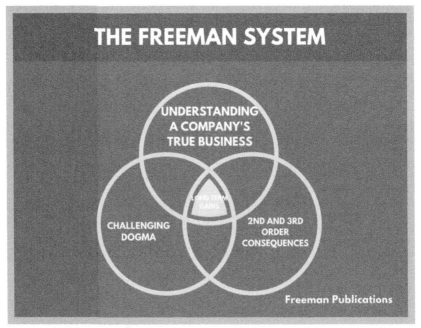

"THERE IS ONLY ONE BOSS. THE CUSTOMER. AND HE CAN FIRE EVERYBODY IN THE COMPANY FROM THE CHAIRMAN ON DOWN, SIMPLY BY SPENDING HIS MONEY SOMEWHERE ELSE."

- Sam Walton

6

THE 20 BEST COMPANIES TO BUY
AND HOLD FOR THE NEXT 20 YEARS

Taking all of the principles we've discussed thus far in mind, here are 20 great companies that meet our criteria. We consider all of them to be great options to buy and hold for the next 20 years. You will have heard of some of these names, while others might be unfamiliar to you. Due to the nature of analyst reports, you will also read mixed reviews of every single company mentioned here. Keep in mind the principles discussed in the previous two chapters when reading about these companies.

DISNEY

Market cap - $188.67 billion

52 week high/low - 153.41/79.07

Disney is one of the companies most affected by the COVID-19 crisis. Its parks have been shut, and direct to consumer sales have dropped significantly. In fact, Disneyland has even been dubbed 'the emptiest place on earth' thanks to the shutdown after the virus pandemic.

There's no denying that Disney faces rough weather over the next 12-18 months. This is primarily because the effects of the virus will spread far and wide. It is gradually becoming clear that the longer it takes to find a cure for it, the worse the economic outlook.

As of this writing, Disney stock has plummeted t0 around $101 from highs of $140 in February. That's a drop of over 25% in less than two months. Market sentiment is bearish. So, why do we think Disney is a great stock to own for the next 20 years?

Parks

While the short term future for Disney's parks and direct to consumer retail businesses is pretty bad, there's no denying that the brand and its intellectual property has a highly sustainable moat. Put it this way: If your child was given a choice of visiting either Disneyland or going to Pete's Fun Park, which one do you think they'd be likely to choose?

Disney has been associated with fun and cartoons for such a long time now that it automatically invokes feelings of childhood when a person hears about it. Despite this strong moat, the company has continuously worked to make the experience at its parks even more enjoyable.

The launch of the PlayDisney Park app turns even longer wait times in lines into a fun experience. This indicates the innovative nature in which the management of the company attacks its weak points. People don't like waiting in long lines. While the PlayDisney Park app may not remove this weakness entirely, it does go a long way towards reducing its negative effects.

Another critical development to watch out for is this: The company has purchased 26 acres of land in Orlando that lie adjacent to the Magic Kingdom, which is one of the oldest Disney parks in the world (Saibil, 2020). This is not the only purchase the company has made. In fact, it happens to be the smallest purchase. Overall, the company has bought close to 5,000 acres of land in an attempt to improve the experience at its parks and resorts. Reinvestment of such scale indicates that management is quite confident of the cash position of the company and are looking to extend their competitive advantage.

DISNEY+

Disney is a lot more than just its parks, even if this is the first association people make. The company is a media conglomerate with its hands in almost everything you can think of. We'll get to the extent to which Disney dominates the media world shortly. For now, the most significant development has been the launch of Disney+, the company's streaming service.

Disney has been seemingly late to the streaming game and on the surface of it, competing against the likes of Netflix and Amazon Prime Video seems like a tough job. However, the company has successfully avoided trying to be a pioneer. Instead choosing to wait for its rivals to work out any kinks in the process.

The success of Disney+ shortly after its launch proves that the strategy has paid off. As of this writing, Disney+ has over 28 million subscribers in the United States alone. In comparison, Netflix has 60 million subscribers despite having been around for more than a decade now.

Given that Disney+ has just launched, this number is only going to grow in size. It isn't just the domestic market that the company has managed to penetrate. With sensible acquisitions of streaming services in emerging markets, the company has managed to gain an outsized footprint in these markets.

A good example of this was the purchase of the Indian streaming app Hotstar. India has one of the highest penetration and usage rates of mobile data in the world. It also happens to have some of the cheapest data plans in the world, and the price is the primary evaluation tool before signing up for any service.

Netflix and Amazon found this out pretty early, and both companies have not made any significant headway in this regard. Netflix currently has just 2 million subscribers in India (Gupta, 2020). In contrast, Disney+, launched via Hotstar, had over 8 million subscribers on day one.

Licensing

A significant chunk of Disney's business comes from the licensing rights it owns for a number of movie franchises and other content. All those Marvel movies that occupied our imagination for over a decade? Disney owned all of them. The Star Wars franchise? Owned by Disney. The company is more than just Mickey Mouse.

The extent of Disney's domination of the entertainment industry is highlighted by the fact that the company owns even smaller animated studios. Pixar is a name that is associated with high-quality animated films and Disney owns the studio outright.

In short, almost all content that is distributed to children is owned by Disney, and this creates a steady and gargantuan revenue stream in form of royalty payments. Imagine writing a book that continues to sell for 100 years, and you simply get to pocket the royalties forever. Now, multiply that by a few billion. That's what Disney is sitting on. That's without taking into account the lifetime customer value of these children as they grow into adulthood and have children of their own. Such is the power of an intangible asset such as nostalgia.

Acquisitions

Disney's most robust quality over time has been the pragmatic nature of its acquisitions. The company has never been shy about acquiring competing businesses and then allow those businesses to have a free hand while under the Disney umbrella. Pixar is a great example of this.

Pixar was originally an upstart competitor that disrupted the traditional Disney animated movie formula. While Disney's movies were epics loaded with songs and all sorts of heavy-handed dialogue (think The Lion King), Pixar's movies were light and still managed to pack a punch to the gut of every adult who watched them.

Conventional wisdom would have dictated that Disney use its significant resources to crush the upstart. However, Disney made the pragmatic choice of simply buying Pixar out and giving it full freedom to whatever it wanted, even if it competed against Disney's non-Pixar animated movies.

A similar example was Disney's acquisition of television networks ABC and ESPN. A first, it seemed that Disney was playing far outside of its field of competence. However, the strategy is quite clear now. Despite there being no link between cartoons and sports, Disney now occupies significant market share in the media sphere, and this almost guarantees the success of its ventures in the entertainment field.

As such, the company is a snowball rolling downhill when it comes to the media and entertainment business. It sustains itself and will continue to do so in the future. This is because its subsidiaries have substantial moats of their own to support themselves.

Issues

These are extraordinary times as you can imagine, and there are significant challenges for Disney to face. The first is the significant loss of income from the park and merchandising business. In 2019, as per Disney's annual report, the company earned over $6.7 billion from these avenues.

In addition to this, it also earned over $2.6 billion from studio revenues. Both of these income streams will be massively affected, thanks to the shutdown. The company does have $12 billion in cash reserves. This ought to be enough to tide the company over any short term crisis, however, replacing close to $9 billion in earnings is going to be pretty tough.

However, Disney is hardly the only company facing such a crisis. Pretty much every single business in the world has to weather the storm. Disney has the luxury of leaning on its media network businesses, which ought to see a rise in earnings as time goes on. As of 2019, this division earned $7.5 billion and was the profit leader for the company.

The short term is uncertain for Disney just as it is for the rest of the world. If we were to bank on human societies figuring out solutions to the current crisis, there is no doubt that Disney is better positioned to bounce back once the tough times pass.

SANDSTORM GOLD

Market cap - $1.01 billion

52 week high/low - 7.90/3.32

Sandstrom Gold is a company not many investors have heard of. It's probably the least well-known company on our list. The company is based out of Canada, and it represents a great way to invest in gold and mining opportunities. The business model of this company is known as gold streaming, and here's how it works.

In the precious metals world, the practice of streaming refers to a company providing financing to a miner or driller. In exchange, the financing company receives the commodity that is being excavated. This practice has long been present in the oil drilling sector, where drillers face huge capital costs and an uncertain, fluctuating market for their goods.

They can spend a lot of money drilling for oil only to find that the market price for oil is low, and this leaves them with a massive hole in their pockets. Drilling for oil takes time and this causes a considerable amount of risk for drillers. This is where the streamer comes in.

The streamer pays the driller cash, and in return, the driller promises to sell the commodity to the streamer for a fixed price. This price is usually a percentage below whatever market value is present at the time.

This makes a lot of sense for the driller since they receive an immediate cash injection. From the streamer's perspective, they're receiving an asset that they can immediately sell back to the market for a profit. They'll need to wait until the resource is available, of course but they don't bare any of the costs of running a mine. A streamer can technically run their business out of their basement.

Gold streamers implement this business model in gold mining, and Sandstorm is one of the standout companies in this regard. The company was founded by

Nolan Watson and David Avram in 2008, right when everything else was falling to pieces. 2009 saw the company ink its first two streaming deals.

Streaming deals take a while to start producing because the miner needs time to extract gold. To cover costs in the short term and to also provide financing for these deals, streamers borrow money from banks. However, due to the lack of cash flow from the mining assets, the company needs to find a way to pay interest on these bank loans. The result is that streamers issue equity or issue debt and bypass banks, to begin with.

There is a risk for shareholders that their shares will be diluted over time thanks to the issue of equity. Thus far, Sandstorm's management has exercised great prudence and has managed its debt to equity mix admirably.

The stock was listed on the NYSE in 2012 and has carried out significant acquisitions since then. As of current writing, the company owns 191 different royalty streams and has a free cash flow of $225 million from 23 different gold mines.

Advantages

So why should you invest in Sandstorm Gold? The more pertinent question to ask is, why should you be investing in gold streaming to begin with? Only once this question has been answered should we even consider Sandstorm as an investment. The first reason to invest in gold streaming is the business model itself.

Streaming companies are essentially a bank as far as miners are concerned. Traditionally, miners had to approach banks for short term loans and place their assets as collateral. This isn't the case when it comes to sourcing financing from streamers. The streamer is a business partner in the deal since they are also exposed to the output from the mine.

This provides miners with a fair source of financing that doesn't strain their balance sheets too much. After all, a miner's financial position is risky, to begin with. Adding interest-based debt is hardly a sensible move. This means that the streaming business model will always be in demand. It has a strong moat, and a miner needing cash injections will always be on the lookout for a good streaming deal.

It isn't easy to become a streamer. While you might think that anyone with oodles of cash can rock up and finance a mine, the reality of the business is quite different. To evaluate the potential of a mine, management needs to have significant experience in the field. They need to have experts on board who can reasonably assess the predicted output of the mine.

Only once this is done can any kind of financing terms be agreed upon. At this point, further experience is needed because there are various ways in which the deal can go wrong. For starters, the streamer needs to have a good idea of future commodity prices. They'll be receiving the commodity in the future, so current prices don't matter.

Next, they need to assess the capabilities of the miner. While the mine may be fit to produce gold, does the miner have enough resources to make this possible? Will the investment be enough, or will the miner need more? These are not easy questions to answer.

Our point is that the business has significant hurdles to jump over, and the economics of it is built for a small number of companies to dominate as long as they have management expertise. The quality of management is the most important thing since there are no traditional assets that the business owns.

However, this is a good thing because the lack of traditional assets means that overhead expenses are low, and as a result, free cash flow levels are high. There are no significant capital expenditures necessary, and this reduces the strain on the company's financials. The only risk to mitigate is the waiting period between providing financing and receiving royalty payments.

As we mentioned earlier, streaming companies need to find ways to raise cash. They do this by either seeking financing from banks themselves or by issuing debt and stock. There are many ways to go wrong here and experience is what counts. This means that a company that has survived and thrived in this business for long is in a much better position to earn a profit and lower their risk than a new company. Experience really does pay off when it comes to streaming.

Thus, when looking for a company to invest in, it pays to evaluate management experience as well as the cash flow qualities of a company. In this regard, Sandstorm checks all boxes.

First, the deals it structures are intelligently done. The company structures what are called NSR deals. NSR stands for net smelter royalties. This means that Sandstorm provides financing based on the output of the mine and not on the viability of mining operations. There is a big distinction between the two. NSR royalties are paid on the basis of the output that comes directly from the ground. This what Sandstorm earns. The miner, on the other hand earns a profit only after they sell the gold to Sandstorm and subtract their own mining costs from this revenue.

In other words, Sandstorm is effectively buying shares in the mine's deposits and isn't concerned with the fortunes of the miner or the miner's operation costs.

It completely cuts Sandstorm's risk in terms of mining operations and ties it directly to the output of the mine. Since this is something that the company can evaluate well, it is playing within its field of knowledge.

Shareholder dilution is a primary concern for any investor and Sandstorm management is on top of this as well. The company has repurchased close to 10 million shares between 2018 to February 2020. With plans to repurchase even more shares given the depressed state of the market.

This shows both confidence in the company's performance as well as a considerable reduction in dilution from an investor's perspective. Given the current industry outlook, Sandstorm Gold is well set to dominate its niche for a long time.

Gold streamers have historically proved to be better investments than traditional gold itself. Gold is often used as a hedge within investor portfolios. If the value of the U.S Dollar decreases, then gold usually witnesses an upswing thanks to the correlation that exists between the two. Gold is viewed as a safe haven in tough times, and this is what causes the upswing in gold prices when the dollar declines in value.

Despite this, gold is a risky investment. Some supply and demand forces apply to it, but it is a tricky thing to predict. Between 2008 and 2018, gold prices rose only by 45%. You'd have thought that gold mining companies would have been able to make money thanks to this, but in fact, their stocks were **down** 38% in this 10 year period.

In contrast, gold streamers' stocks rose by an astronomical 189% during this time. A significant reason for this is all of the factors that we outlined previously. A built-in profit margin and low overheads turbocharge investment returns, and this is reflected in the rise in stock prices.

WALMART

Market cap - $344.97 billion

52 week high/low - 128.08/96.79

Walmart is one of the mainstays of the American retail space. Industry experts have always worried about the ability of the company to overcome challenges, but the fact is that the company is still standing. More importantly, it has survived the gargantuan challenge that Amazon poses.

Amazon has succeeded in wiping out almost every retailer in America and continues to do so around the world, wherever it decides to enter. The fact is that not only has Walmart survived Amazon and the digital revolution, but it has also barely felt the impact of it. This is because it has a significant moat.

You might think that the brand name is what sustains it, but the real moat that Walmart has significant economies of scale. Its sheer size allows for it to take more substantial risks and reduce the economic impact of taking such risks. This, in turn, enables the company to achieve huge consumer satisfaction levels.

Recession-Proof

The advantage that Walmart's moat gives it is that it is practically recession-proof. This was one of the few companies that actually managed to thrive during the economic crisis of the previous decade. Think about it: When times are tough, the first place you think about when it comes to grocery shopping is Walmart.

The current crisis will most likely lead to a recession. With more than 33 million unemployed in the US, the economic impact of COVID-19 is being felt far and wide. While Walmart's physical stores might be closed, its online delivery system is in full swing. We'll address this shortly. As of now, keep in mind that stores cannot remain closed forever.

Despite the challenges the COVID-19 virus brings, at some point, people are going to have to go back outside and buy groceries. When they do, they're going to have less money on average than before, and the first place they'll head to is Walmart. The store stocks virtually everything you can think of, and if saving money is the top priority, this is the place to head to.

Perhaps the biggest strength of Walmart is that 56% of its sales come directly from groceries and food sales. As you can imagine, the demand for this is unlikely to dampen anytime soon. The market prices of Walmart reflect this. While 2020 has been massively bearish for stocks as a whole, with the S&P 500 declining by 30%, Walmart stock declined by just 3.8% overall.

Not only is the company robust in tough times, but its stock also holds up pretty well, too.

Management Philosophy

Sam Walton was one of the first people to make economies of scale a business policy actively. What we mean by this is that while other retailers at the time focused on stocking goods and serving local customers, Walton realized the power of a chain store model where sheer size could allow him to dictate prices to his suppliers and thereby drive costs down.

This allowed him to open several small stores at first and essentially encircle his competitors. When it comes to shopping items such as groceries, consumers are incredibly price-conscious for the most part. Achieving economies of scale allowed Walton to address his consumers' biggest need directly.

Consider that Walton managed to go from running a single store in Arkansas to running a billion-dollar company within his lifetime, and you'll see the power of his business model.

One of Walton's greatest innovations was to locate his stores in small towns at first instead of large cities. Conventional wisdom at the time was to locate big stores in big cities and smaller ones in small towns, thanks to smaller populations. Walton's large stores managed to dominate not just a single town but the entire area around it. What's more, the presence of Walmart discouraged anyone else from entering and thereby reduced competition.

Another innovation he pioneered was to insist on fast logistics. He did this by locating Walmart supply centers at less than an hour's drive away from his stores and insisted on Walmart's fleet of trucks supplying the stores to ensure speedy delivery of goods. This way, Walmart was assured of its prime position in the market.

This policy continues to this day. If anything, Walmart's practices have only become stronger since the founder's death. Warren Buffett is just one of many notable investors who made mention of this in 2006. Walton's legacy lives on in his book, *Sam Walton: Made in America*, which continues to be one of the best business books ever written.

The principles that Sam Walton instilled in his company created a massive advantage for them, and it continues to power the corporation to this day.

E-commerce

Walmart has always been thought of as being late to the e-commerce game. However, in our opinion, this was simply the firm doubling down on its already strong business model and expanding only when it made sense. The majority of

Walmart's sales come from small towns to this day, and consumers in those markets do not traditionally purchase goods online.

This behavior is changing, and Walmart has responded brilliantly to it. As of this writing, online ordering and kerbside pickup is available in 60% of its stores. With this number projected to increase to 90% by the end of 2021. Despite this seemingly late entry into e-commerce, Walmart is still alive, while the majority of its competition is dying with e-commerce companies facing a raft of bank-ruptcies.

Most telling is the behavior of the giant that killed the competition: Amazon. Consider the fact that Amazon operates a very similar business model to Walmart but does it in the online space. It makes sense for Amazon to enter the low-cost grocery and essentials market.

Yet Amazon resists doing so. The company instead chose to buy premium grocer Whole Foods instead of trying to compete with Walmart in the budget grocery space. The fact that Amazon shied away from a direct confrontation is pretty telling. It communicates to investors that Walmart, despite all the gripes about the company being stuck in the past, is firmly entrenched in the hearts and minds of its customer base.

Walmart has expanded significantly abroad and has made repeated forays into the market that suits its business model the best: India. The government of India had to pass laws guarding the interests of small shopkeepers once news broke that Walmart was considering Indian investment. While it was a setback to the company, this event once again shows how pretty much no one wants to compete against this behemoth.

As of now, Walmart is operating in the country as a wholesaler. However, its biggest move there has been to acquire a portion of Amazon's Indian rival Flip-kart for $16 billion. The move initially didn't make sense, but there are clearly echoes of its earlier investment in Chinese company JD.com in the Flipkart deal.

In China, Walmart operates online stores for small retailers as well as some of its competitors, such as British grocery chain Asda. In bigger cities, Walmart also runs hybrid online and offline retail stores where customers can scan and go. Clearly, Walmart's move into the developing world is putting it ahead of the curve of many of its competitors.

The company is willing to go to any market as long as the terms of the deal are right. This could be in India or Vietnam. It doesn't matter. Its strong balance sheet and hoards of cash ensure that Walmart will always remain in a strong position for the future.

Brand Value

The economies of scale that Walmart has pushed its brand value to stratospheric heights. This is a unique occurrence when it comes to chain stores. Every chain store retailer struggles against the brands it sells in terms of name recognition. For example, people know what Nordstrom is, but why would they go to Nordstrom in a mall that has Gucci and Versace stores as well?

However, this is not the case with Walmart. Consider this scenario: Let's say there's a brand of cheap cereal that is available for the same price at Luke's Groceries and Walmart. Where will people go? Most likely Walmart. Even if the cereal company decides to sell exclusively to Luke's Groceries, people will still flock to Walmart because that's where you get all kinds of cheap stuff.

By choosing not to sell their product in Walmart, the cereal company is effectively removing itself out of its customers' reach. It's saying that it isn't a budget brand anymore. In other words, it would be suicide for them to do this. This illustrates the moat that the Walmart brand has.

A similar phenomenon exists with its big-box retail outlet, Sam's Club too.

All in all, the stock is not one of those high flying or sexy stocks that you can boast about owning. However, when it comes down to it, Walmart has all the qualities you look for in a good company and a stock that you want to hold onto for the rest of your life.

MCDONALD'S

Market cap - $136.94 billion

52 week high/low - 221.93/124.23

McDonald's might not be your preferred option when it comes to eating out, but this doesn't mean it's a bad investment. In fact, it might be one of the best investments you can find right now. First off is its track record. The reason McDonald's has always performed well is due to its robust business model. We highlighted this in an example previously and will delve into it shortly in more detail.

The company has an enviable track record when it comes to providing shareholders with value. McDonald's is a dividend aristocrat. This moniker is bestowed upon companies that have consistently made and increased dividend payments every year for the past 25 years. This is not an easy achievement, and it further indicates McDonald's' ability to weather crises.

Then there's the appeal of the fast-food chain. Generally speaking, in recessions or downturns, fast food chains tend to perform well since they're a source of cheap and quick food. Sit-down restaurants tend to struggle in contrast.

What's more, McDonald's has also invested significant sums into reducing costs even further by investing in AI and technology when it comes to the ordering process. There's no denying that the COVID-19 prompted lockdowns have heavily hit the restaurant industry. People are staying and eating at home more than ever. Therefore, it is worth analyzing how McDonald's is positioned regarding the immediate crisis as well as the repercussions of it that will occur down the road.

Current Impact

Let's begin by taking a look at how badly operations have been hit due to lockdowns and closures of locations. In this regard, McDonald's has suffered, but it hasn't been as bad as you might initially think. This is because of three major factors that it has going for it. The first is the way the business is structured.

McDonald's is in the real estate business as much as it is in the restaurant business. The company owns all of its locations and leases them out to franchisees for a high markup. This means that the company is guaranteed cash flow every month to a much higher degree than its competition.

As of current writing, as much as 85% of its outlets are franchisee operated. This means that the large majority of its locations are regular cash producers and the risk of the shutdown is primarily outsourced to the franchisees. While the company has announced plans to work with franchisees, the failure of a single franchisee simply means that there's someone else to occupy the place. After all, the location itself isn't in jeopardy. While there will be a short term cash hit, this has little relevance to the long term viability of the business.

Another advantage of this business model is that the company operates its restaurants at far lower costs than its competitors do. After all, it doesn't bear any expense when it comes to utility bills or any other rental expense. The franchisee takes the costs throughout. In return, McDonald's lends them the weight of their brand name and a large cut of revenues.

The second advantage is that the emphasis on fast food has allowed McDonald's to build drive-thru outlets as well as implement a range of AI-powered ordering systems in its stores. For example, in specific locations in China, there is no need for a customer to interact with a human being. They simply walk up and place their order at a terminal and receive their food.

Drive-thrus are witnessing a huge leap forward thanks to self-isolation measures, and until a vaccine is found for the virus, this state of things is likely to remain. In 2019, McDonald's reported that 65% of its sales in the U.S came from drive-thrus. This number is only going to increase. This means that the closure of seating areas are unlikely to have too much of a negative impact on earnings.

Another great move the company had previously taken was to partner with food delivery firms. Critics pointed out that McDonald's didn't have a dedicated partner, but, to be honest, this just reflects the fact that there isn't a single company that has been able to dominate the niche. McDonald's's decision to partner with different firms is simply the company diversifying its risk across partners.

As of now, there are no predictions that can possibly quantify exact numbers from the effect this move has had. However, these factors make it likely that the negative impact of the virus will be blunted quite a bit when it comes to McDonald's.

Recession Impact

The economic impact of the virus is already being felt in the U.S. Unemployment numbers now top 33 million, and many businesses show no signs of immediate recovery. All of this points to the fact that there will be a recession. A bad one. So, how is McDonald's poised to perform during these times? For starters, being a cheap fast food restaurant is going to work in its favor in the majority of the world. People are unlikely to stop eating McDonald's just because times are rough. If anything, the opposite is the case.

Looking at the company's performance in prior recessions is instructive. In the crisis of 2008, the company managed to increase its revenues every year from 2007 until 2011. The same happened once the dotcom bubble burst around 2000. McDonald's increased its revenues like clockwork from 1999 until 2001.

An important point to note is that earnings growth rates didn't match sales growth during these periods. This indicates that the company reduced its margins, but given the economic conditions, this is an understandable move. All of this points to the fact that McDonald's is well poised to handle the upcoming economic recession, should it ever occur.

Financial Strength

This is where things get a little risky with McDonald's. At the end of 2019, thanks to major investments in technology and other assets, the company's cash position was low. As soon as the lockdowns started hitting, this low cash position became an even bigger concern thanks to the decrease in revenues.

This prompted the company to withdraw its $1 billion credit facility. A credit facility is like an overdraft account that companies can borrow from. However, the fact remains that it has $34 billion in debt on its balance sheet, with $6 billion coming due in 2023. This payment might prove to be problematic for management.

There are no easy solutions for its debt problem, despite experts noting that it fully expects McDonald's to pull through this time. However, companies the size of McDonald's have greater power to renegotiate payment terms and kick the can down the road until a moment when revenues stabilize. This is likely to with the 2023 payment.

This year is going to be a tough one for McDonald's as it will be for the rest of the world. How well the business model manages to support McDonald's remains to be seen. There's no doubt that it will ensure that McDonald's navigates these times with more certainty than its peers.

Another important factor to consider when it comes to McDonald's is its dividend's status. Any suspension of a dividend will result in it losing the aristocrat label, and this will result in a downward plunge in stock prices.

As of this writing, the company has suspended its stock buyback program. This is probably in order to save cash for the dividend payment and to increase it by marginal amounts. Generally speaking, the company has weathered crises in the past, and as such, one can expect it to pull through, even though the short term picture is uncertain.

Bottom Line

The company's biggest issue happens to be its high levels of debt which has placed it in a tricky situation right before an unforeseeable crisis. Despite this, it is well placed to handle tough times. Even if the worst does happen and earnings plummet, the company is still a real estate giant that owns all of its properties.

It is not going to lose locations just because it cannot pay the rent. It is free to find different ways to boost revenues, and the increased cash flow will enable it to survive on shoestring margins. Think of it this way: As long as it pays all of its creditors, does the existence of a profit matter all that much? We're not saying that the company will deliberately run a loss.

The point is that even the worst-case scenario is not going to result in as much pain as some of its competitors will feel during the next few years. All of this makes McDonald's a safe haven stock that is most likely going to be around and thrive for a very long time.

MARKEL

Market cap - $13.86 billion

52 week high/low - 1347.64/710.52

Typing Markel into Google usually results in the search engine asking you if you meant to type 'marvel' instead. This is a pretty apt way to describe what Markel is all about. It is one of the biggest companies on the planet no one knows, and this is a very good thing. Markel has been dubbed 'the baby Berkshire' due to the similarity between the way it is structured.

Markel is an insurance giant, and it began its life as a specialty insurance company for long haul truckers and jitney buses in the 1930s. Specialty insurance is an excellent field for many companies to carve a moat in because the number of customers that require such insurance is low, and any company that can successfully underwrite policies tends to be quite successful.

The insurance business itself is an immensely profitable one, and it is one that a lot of professional investors seek to get into. The famed founder of Stansberry Research, Porter Stansberry, once quipped that insurance was the one business that he would teach his children. Despite this, the average investor doesn't truly understand the power of the business. In order to fully understand the potential of Markel, we need to first examine how the insurance industry works and why it is so desirable.

An insurance company writes policy and receives premium payments like clockwork in return for promising to pay a sum in case things go wrong. The sum that needs to be paid is usually far more than the premium that is charged. The insurer's job is to figure out how much risk they're running on the policy and accordingly price their premiums. However, they can't price them too high because their competitors might undercut them.

If a policy expires and the company has to never payout, this creates what is called an underwriting profit for the company. An underwriting profit is a unicorn for insurance companies since they're notoriously difficult to come by. It's tough to predict risk after all, and at some point, the insurer has to pay out the amount for which the policy is insured.

This is why most insurance companies don't even try to earn an underwriting profit. Instead, they aim to breakeven or even run a loss in order to simply capture market share and keep the cash flow levels high. Now, there is usually some period of time between receiving premium payments and having to pay out the insured sum.

For example, you make health insurance payments every month, but it's not as if you're going to claim benefits every single month. You'll most likely claim them at some point down the road. During this time, the insurance company gets to keep your cash without any obligation to return it. This money is called float.

If the company manages to secure an underwriting profit, it creates a free float. In essence, a free-float is simply free money. Insurance companies that don't generate a free float can still earn a profit. They do this by investing the float into the market. In short, they act as fund managers and aim to generate returns with all the cash that they have lying around.

Many insurance companies rely on generating profits with the float they have instead of underwriting. The best companies such as Berkshire Hathaway and

Markel tend to produce both investment returns as well as underwriting profits. This creates a free-float that effectively leverages their investments.

Think of it in this way. Let's say you buy stock A for $100 and it pays you $25 in cash dividends. You reinvest this $25 into another stock B that pays you $10 in cash. You reinvest $10 into C that pays you $2 and so on until you're invested in a number of stocks. However, your original investment amount is still $100. You've turned $100 into an investment into at least four stocks that have spawned even more investments.

Float creates leverage as well, but since this isn't free money, the overall returns are hampered a bit. The company needs to pay this amount back at some point since their customers will make claims on their policies. In essence, the float a company carries is a short term loan to the insurer, and a free float is a loan that never has to be paid back.

Markel is one of those insurers that understands the power of cash flow and practices this with its own investments.

Quality of Investments

Markel's portfolio over the years has reflected management's philosophy that businesses that generate a high degree of cash flow are the best ones to invest in. In fact, management is so confident in their ability to pick investments that they don't pay dividends, which is unusual amongst insurers.

Typically, the free cash flow that an insurer generates is returned to the shareholders since the company cannot find adequate uses for it. However, Markel has successfully used its free-float and cash flow to increase its holdings in its portfolio and deliver even greater returns to its shareholders.

Shareholder Base

When speaking of Markel, special mention must be made of the quality of the shareholder base that the company has. The company seems to have a high number of shareholders who are focused on capturing long term gains through their investment and, as such, are willing to stomach a few negative quarters or two.

I say quarters and not years here because the average public company faces intense scrutiny after a few quarters of losses. Wall Street gangs up on them and this forces management to place short term results above long term growth as we explained previously.

This is not the case at Markel since there aren't any agitators present. As such, the company is run like a private company. Where the business aims are aligned with the long term growth of the company.

Niche

Property and casualty insurance remains the primary driver of the business, and these are great niches for Markel to operate in. This is because the company faces little competition and it has a great deal of pricing power. This is a direct result of excellent customer service and competitive pricing that keeps competitors out as well as ensures a moat for the company.

Reinsurance

It's not all great news with Markel, and there are some risks you need to be aware of. All of these risks typically center around the reinsurance business. Reinsurance is insurance for insurance companies. For example, if insurance company A decides that it has some pretty risky contracts on its books, it approaches a reinsurer to insure those contracts.

As you can imagine, reinsurance is a pretty risky business. The biggest risk here is the fact that all of the situations that the company has to insure are so-called long-tail situations. A long-tail refers to the fact that payouts can occur many years into the future, and when they do, they tend to be substantial.

Thus, a reinsurer can carry a huge amount of risk on their books without ever knowing the true cost of the policy until the time comes, if it ever does, to pay. Typically, reinsurance policies are sought for extreme events such as a global pandemic like the one we're living through right now.

How does one estimate the odds of a disease spreading like wildfire? Furthermore, how does one even begin to calculate the economic impact of such pandemics? It depends on the disease of course. How can anyone predict what kind of a disease might occur next? These are impossible questions to answer.

Reinsurance company underwriters thus need to be masters of risk management, and they need some luck on their side as well. For the most part, reinsurers generate high levels of free float, but when they do find themselves in a position of having to pay, they end up draining their cash reserves and going into the red. The levels of losses they typically sustain cannot be compensated by the returns they receive from the free float.

Even the esteemed Berkshire Hathaway has been burned at the reinsurance game a few times, and Markel is no exception. Insurance companies use a metric called the combined ratio to calculate their profit and loss levels. This is calculated by dividing the total expenses and losses incurred by the premiums earned.

The smaller the number is, the greater the profit is. Markel's combined ratio for 2019 was a healthy 93%. This means that expenses were 93% of premiums earned which means they earned a good amount of free float. However, this clouds the fact that the company's reinsurance division posted a ratio of 120%.

It was property and casualty that brought that number down to 93%. You might wonder why a company would even consider entering the reinsurance game if it's so risky. Well, it has to do with the rewards on offer. It's a bit like asking why would you borrow money to buy a home. The value of the asset and security makes up for it.

The prospect of the value of the home decreasing is just a risk you have to take. It's the same with the reinsurance business. Having said all of this about Markel's reinsurance business, it must be noted that the managers of the company have wisely minimized the effect of it on their overall portfolio.

If a 120% combined ratio in reinsurance still results in 93% overall combined ratio, then this is a risk that the company can justifiably take.

Smart management and a carefully engineered moat make Markel is a fantastic company for the long term and a great addition to any portfolio.

STARBUCKS

Market cap - $86.71 billion

52 week high/low - 99.72/50.02

Starbucks has been an interesting case study to evaluate how companies will perform during these tough times. This is because the two biggest markets for Starbucks happen to be the US and China. Given the global situation, Starbucks was one of the first major companies to get hit with store closures and self-isolation measures.

Given that the Chinese situation is ahead of the rest of the world at the moment, in terms of recovery, the initial for Starbucks made for interesting reading. First off, the company announced that while sales dropped disastrously during the first quarter of 2020, there was a growth in-store visits as lockdown curbs eased.

The picture isn't all that great, but it does prove that the business model of Starbucks is still very much viable. The company might be in the coffee shop business on the surface but its real appeal lies in the fact that it is a great third space for people to meet. Whether it is to meet for a date or a business meeting or even sit and work, Starbucks is an obvious choice for most people.

The company is coming up on its 50th anniversary next year and in 2019, it opened 1,439 new stores worldwide. As the year ended, the company reported an increase in same-store sales to the tune of three percent. Then the virus hit and things took a turn for the worse. The biggest gripe about Starbucks, from people who don't understand the business, is the fact that it has always been a bit too luxurious a brand to appeal to people during a recession.

The price of a single cup of Starbucks coffee has always been on the higher side. Paying $5 for a single cup does sound ridiculous when compared to its competition but people pay this amount for much more than just the coffee. The ordering experience and ambiance are what people *really* pay for.

There are a number of factors that ensure that Starbucks is well placed to handle the tough times ahead.

Brand Loyalty

As we just mentioned, people who drink Starbucks coffee usually drink only Starbucks coffee. The addition of food options to the menu in recent years and the general ambiance of their locations means that customers tend to return to the location more often than not.

Starbucks is one of those rare companies that rewards its customers back once they're shown loyalty. The rewards program is one of the most generous and is a drawing point for many new customers. Apart from having the ability to order ahead of time, rewards program customers also receive free refills of hot coffee or tea in-store.

Customers in higher tiers receive free snacks and food as well, and this guarantees that they'll always be back to visit. All in all, the company has brand loyalty figured out really well, and this will keep it in good standing through tough times. On the surface of it, closure of shop locations will hurt sales. However, once lockdown curbs ease, people will be keen on socializing once more.

Given the negative impact on their wallets, spending $5 for a cup of coffee and chatting at a Starbucks is a pretty cheap way to socialize. The coffee might be expensive, but the purpose of a customer's visit isn't to just have a cup of coffee.

Prior Experience

Much like with McDonald's, it's instructive to take a look at how Starbucks managed to handle the previous recessions. Here, there isn't as much of a track record we have to play with. The previous recession coincided with the business model of Starbucks circling the drain as well. The company was in trouble headed into the recession and the crisis only made things worse.

The return of Howard Schultz, the founder, as CEO helped get things back on track. Starbucks embarked on an unprecedented program of winning back its customers' trust. It began with a series of surveys and questions that the company asked its customers concerning the customer experience.

The response was tremendous and the company carried out many of the recommendations that its customers wanted. It remained one of the few instances when a large public corporation gave its customers free rein when it comes to suggesting improvements and directing the course of the company. All of this helped Starbucks exit the crisis in much better shape than how it entered it.

Will the same experience help the company this time around? The exact steps it took last time might not apply during these times because the nature of the crisis is different. During 2008, customers were dissatisfied while this time around, this doesn't appear to be the case.

What will stand the company in good stead is that its focus on customer loyalty has paid off massively, and this has led to a strong brand presence. This is a very good thing when it comes to handling tough times. While there's no way to predict how the company will handle the recession, its focus on its customers does put it in a good place.

Diversification

While the brick and mortar locations remain Starbucks' primary earners, the company has been diversifying to create additional revenue streams. One of the side effects of brand loyalty and recognition that was born from the previous crisis is that it enabled the company to sell its brand of coffee in supermarkets.

This brought in a decent chunk of cash, and while this isn't nearly enough to sustain the company all by itself, it does dampen the negative impact quite a bit. In addition to this, Starbucks has partnered with several delivery companies and has been expanding its drive-thru and mobile ordering platforms.

All of these platforms will see increased consumer interaction as buying habits chance post this crisis.

All in all, despite having many factors working against it, Starbucks is a company that is poised to break out once the lockdowns end, and people begin to adjust to the new economic and social reality that the virus will bring about. The short term might be painful for investors, but the long term does promise stable growth.

CROWN CASTLE INTERNATIONAL

Market cap - $68.41 billion

52 week high/low - 168.75/114.18

Crown Castle is a relatively unknown stock thanks to the fact that it happens to be a real estate investment trust or a REIT. These companies don't have to pay corporate taxes but are obligated to return 90% of their profits to their share-holders in return. Typically REITs invest in real estate assets and make money by managing those properties.

REITs have become increasingly popular over the past five years. Crown Castle is a specialized REIT that doesn't invest in the usual residences or commercial spaces that are associated with these instruments.

Instead, Crown Castle is a cell phone tower REIT. As the name suggests, the company owns a number of cell phone towers around the country and also manages miles of fiber optic cables that enable communication. In short, this company is a service provider to one of the fastest-growing phenomenon in the world currently: The internet of things.

This phrase is used to signify the increasing degree to which everything in our lives is connected to one another. Each day witnesses new smart devices being launched and the day isn't far off when our vehicles will be able to communicate with our devices at home and exchange data. Wearable tech such as the Fitbit and other smartwatches have witnessed huge increases in demand during this decade and this will only continue to grow. The IoT economy is projected to reach up to $11 Trillion by 2025.

All of these devices need one thing in common: A network. To be precise, they need a network that can handle the increasing number of connections and data being exchanged. This data will need to be transmitted faster and with more efficiency than current networks can handle. Communications protocols aren't far behind at the moment.

4G networks were a huge step forward in terms of reducing latency (the delay between sending data and receiving it), but they cannot handle the rate at which connections are increasing. 5G communication networks are already being set up and the world needs the faster speeds that 5G promises.

While more research is needed, the fact is that existing communication towers and infrastructure are capable of handling 5G's demands. With the number of people connected to the internet only set to increase, communications businesses are a great bet for the future.

This is where cell phone tower REITs come in. These companies earn income by leasing towers to operators and earn a steady income for the lease period. On average, the lease period lasts for five years. In addition to this, these companies also lease their fiber-optic communications facilities to network providers for a fee.

All in all, the future is bright for the industry. The question is, why is Crown Castle the best bet of the lot?

REIT Structure

The first cell phone tower company to convert itself into a REIT was American Tower. This is the best known company of its kind, and since 2011, which is when it became a REIT, the company's stock has returned well in excess of 300% (DiLallo, 2019).

Crown Castle turned itself into a REIT in 2014 and since then has returned 140% for its shareholders. While AMT is the more prominent company, Crown Castle happens to have far better growth prospects. What's more, since it's a REIT, it is legally obligated to pay out 90% of its income to its shareholders.

This means that its dividend yield is higher than the average dividend-paying stock.

As of current writing, the yield on Crown Castle is 3.05%, which is double the size of American Tower's yield. This makes the company an income earner as well as a capital gains machine.

Infrastructure

Currently, almost all of Crown Castle's infrastructure is located in the United States which means it has a stable business environment to work in and doesn't need to worry about international laws and licensing. This is in contrast to American Tower, which operates internationally.

A third cell tower REIT, SBA Communications is also operating internationally thanks to saturation in the American market. This is good news for Crown Castle since its existing infrastructure is unlikely to be disrupted anytime soon.

The company, as of December 2019, has 40,000 towers and 80,000 miles of fiber networks. The business is simple to understand. There are just two divisions: Towers and cable. Operating costs are low and are usually front-loaded when networks and towers need to be installed and brought online.

These costs are typically lowered by adding more tenants to existing infrastructure and thereby reducing unit costs. The addition of more tenants usually boosts operating cash flows quite a bit because costs are low, to begin with, and they dramatically reduce once this happens.

40% of gross income from the towers segment is derived from the land that the company owns. As for the remaining 60%, the average remaining life on the land leases are 35 years long. The largest cell phone companies in America account for 75% of revenues, and there isn't any danger of default with regards to payments. As of now, the towers division is the primary earner with 67% of income derived from it.

As of 2019, the company has invested money into developing its fiber business and they expect income to rise in forthcoming years. Given the demand that 5G is going to place on fiber networks, this seems like a reasonable assumption to make.

Cash Flow Growth

Crown Castle is one of those companies that is poised to make huge growth. As of this writing, the company is about half the size of its competitors but owns a wide variety of great assets across the United States. According to the company's latest annual report, 71% of Crown Castle's towers and fiber networks are present in major business areas around the country.

Given the increase in demand that 5G will bring and the high quality of its assets, investors can expect high levels of cash flow from the company. As such, cash flow has grown at a faster pace thus far when compared to its competitors. A lot of this has to do with the smaller size, and investors cannot expect the same growth rates as the company gets bigger.

However, there is a significant runway for the stock to grow. And the economics of its business seems to be lining up well in this regard.

Risks

No investment is without risk, and Crown Castle has inadvertently stumbled upon a huge risk thanks to the current political climate. 5G finds itself at the heart of the US-China trade war because of the potential it has to unlock greater levels of data transfer. As such, China is considered to be the leader in developing 5G technology, and one firm is the leader when it comes to developing electronic equipment that suits 5G.

This company is Huawei, which found itself being accused of being a spy front for the Chinese government. Right now, Huawei is banned from conducting business in America, and American companies cannot supply or use any of their products. However, this is not the case worldwide.

European governments, in particular have had no qualms about installing Huawei equipment and have resisted American attempts to move away from the company's products. It doesn't help that there isn't a single American company that has the capabilities to develop these products.

The Trump administration, and the Chinese government, view 5G as being the key to global dominance. Given China's massive investments in this technology, it could conceivably dominate the market, and this will result in every technology company using Chinese products to transfer data and conduct business. This is where allegations of spying come from (Rydon, 2020).

While the specifics of the trade war are immaterial here, what investors should keep in mind is that there are likely to be second-order effects on cell tower REITs such as Crown Castle. At this point, we can't predict what these effects will be, but unforeseen circumstances might impact their business.

Right now, the major American carriers have stated that they do not use or plan to use Huawei or Chinese products in their 5G infrastructure. Given that 5G has barely been rolled out as yet, this claim will be tested in the coming years. Will Crown need to upgrade its infrastructure? Will it need to invest more in installing fiber networks? There is a significant risk here to cash flow growth.

This is not to say that the company is going to make a loss due to these risks. After all, 5G demands pretty much the same infrastructure as 4G does. You can think of both networks via an analogy: 4G is a collegiate swimmer while 5G is Micheal Phelps at his prime. The latter is a lot faster, but ultimately, both of them swim in the same pool. Crown Castle is the pool in this case.

A bigger risk to the company than the trade war is the fact that 70% of its revenues come from the major carriers. Any consolidation of these networks is going to reduce its earnings. In fact, T-Mobile and Sprint agreed to merge in 2018 and are in the process of completing the merger. While the impact on Crown's revenues won't be as large, there will be some decrease as overlapping networks get eliminated.

Companies such as Crown tend to grow via acquisition for the most part and disruption to revenues might impact this. While the company has enough cash to fuel growth, it might find that acquisition is not the most practical thing for it to do. Given that there are no other ways for it to grow, this puts it in a sticky situation.

We say that there are no other ways to grow because practically speaking, it takes time to buy land and to erect a tower manually. While a company spends a few months doing this, a competitor can go out and buy another company and instantly add a few 100 towers to its portfolio.

Despite these risks, the quality of Crown Castle's management and its track record proves that the company can weather these storms. The growth in cash flow and the upcoming demand for 5G is certain to fuel overall growth, and Crown is in pole position to lead the way in this sector.

AMAZON

Market cap - $1.19 trillion

52 week high/low - 2475.95/1626.03

From a company very few have heard of, we move onto a company that even your technophobic grandma has heard of. Amazon is everywhere these days, and that is not an understatement. It has become the second company to reach the one trillion-dollar market valuation mark and joined Apple at this spot.

Amazon started off as an online bookseller but has since taken that business model and has replicated it over and over. It begins by raising a war chest through financing. In its earlier days, it did this by venture capital funding. Once this was done, it slashed prices to such an extreme that the competition was forced to quit or risk bankruptcy.

Having gained close to complete market share, the company then consolidates and adds other products to its offerings and generates more lines of cash flow. In its early days, Amazon was all about cash flow and not earnings. In fact, it took Amazon a long time to post a profit, and the business model was questioned widely at the time. The logic was simple. As long as Amazon could fund its expansion with other people's money (venture capital or equity and loans at low-interest rates), and it could pay its expenses, profits didn't matter.

Profits would eventually come when the company reached a specific size where customers would automatically turn to it. This model has repeated over and over again with every single business Amazon enters. The second major business the company entered was IT infrastructure with Amazon Web Services or AWS.

AWS offers cloud-based data centers and a number of large companies such as Zoom and Slack use it as part of their daily business needs. As Amazon expanded into more product segments, the same formula was applied over and over, and gradually, the older business segments began turning a profit.

Today, as the company continues to expand, it doesn't need to raise additional cash because its existing lines of business provide it with all the cash flow it needs. It has even helped Jeff Bezos fund personal investments such as buying the Washington Post newspaper and founding a space rocket company.

Product Lines

Amazon these days has a wide and varied product line. The most prominent one is Prime membership, and this is effectively a loyalty program. Prime member-ship gives its customers access to discounted rates and offers on a number of products and also includes Prime TV access which is Amazon's streaming service.

The company has stayed true to its roots in book retailing and has a vast library of eBooks and paperbacks. Amazon's self-publishing platform incentivizes self-publishers to churn out hundreds of thousands of ebooks every year, and with the acquisition of Audible, Amazon has diversified its book offerings. All of these platforms represent a source of recurring revenues for Amazon.

Amazon's technological forays include developing the Echo home device with its assistant Alexa. This helps amazon collect all kinds of data about consumer behavior that helps tailor product recommendations on the platform.

In addition to this, Amazon has expanded into the grocery business by buying Whole Foods and developing its own pay and go stores. To help support these stores, Amazon has developed a patented Just Walk Out or JWO technology that is still in its early stages of maturity.

As of now, the only customers for this tech are Amazon's own stores, but in the future, it isn't inconceivable to see it spread to smaller and medium-sized retailers everywhere.

Financials

In its early days, Amazon's financials were under constant scrutiny and justifiably so. Bezos' strategy of minimizing earnings at the expense of cash flow was risky, but it paid off. The margin of error was small, but to his credit, he pulled it off, and Amazon is now well within safe territory.

The firm has a good amount of cash, and given the events of the crisis, it should only see increased activity on its website. Amazon is already the biggest shopping search engine on the planet, and this number is only going to grow. What's more, its free cash flow (which is the cash left over after all operating expenses and investments are deducted) has also steadily increased since 2017, which indicates that a number of its internal investments are nearing maturity.

This means the company can expect an earnings boost in the upcoming decade. The sheer extent of the number of products it offers as well as the multiple businesses it is involved in making sure that Amazon is going to find it close to impossible to fail.

IMPACT OF COVID-19

Amazon has not been spared from the impact that the virus has had on the world. The primary casualty has been the delivery services that are offered with Prime membership. Typically, members receive their orders the very next day. However, with the crisis unfolding, Prime orders are being delayed by up to a month.

Amazon has made it clear that they are prioritizing the shipping of essential items above all else. This is probably what has led to alarming sounding numbers like that, but there is no doubt negative impact at the moment. Given its sheer size, one would expect Amazon to recover in short order.

Given the changing behavior of consumers that once can expect in these times, the development of JWO is great news for the company. While its competitors, such as Walmart and Target are unlikely to implement it thanks to data sharing concerns, Amazon is likely going to find several businesses interested in the software. It helps minimize human contact and removes the need for workers to be in harm's way.

The other line of business that is likely maturing at just the right time is digital advertising. As Amazon's platform has grown, it's advertising services have famously lagged. For the longest time, Amazon's marketing services AMS was the most unsophisticated platform when compared to Facebook or Google's platforms.

This has changed rapidly over the past two years, with digital revenues now significant enough to warrant a mention on the quarterly earnings call. As more shoppers turn to Amazon, targeted advertising offers a great way to boost earnings, and here, Amazon is primed to take advantage.

Management

Amazon's success is often ascribed to its CEO Bezos and this is largely true. His management style has been described as prickly and lacking in any sort of empathy. However, his results speak for themselves, and to his credit, Bezos has never been involved in any scandal or dishonest business practice during his career.

Bezos' vision is what ultimately drives Amazon and forms the biggest reason to invest in the company. Much like how Steve Jobs was Apple's biggest economic moat while he was alive, Bezos has created a similar situation for himself and his company.

While he isn't the most forthcoming with his vision, it is safe to say that he has built enough of a track record to justify investing in Amazon. Warren Buffett seems to think so as well with his recent investment in the company. Despite his dubious record when it comes to managing his own employees' wishes, there is no denying that Bezos places customer satisfaction at the top of his list and is willing to go to any extent to satisfy their concerns.

In fact, Bezos has managed to create a truly unique economic moat for his company, and it is one that few other CEOs have succeeded at creating.

Diversified Moat

Given that Amazon straddles so many different lines of business, it is staggering to think of how varied and diversified its moat is. The first and most apparent moat it has is its economies of scale. Amazon is so large and their pockets are so deep that they can afford to drive prices as low as possible and still make a profit.

This is impossible to match, and perhaps Walmart is the only other company on the planet that can do this in the consumer goods segment. However, Amazon does this with every product on its platform. A side effect of this is that it manages to generate large user numbers.

With a large number of users comes data, and this is at the heart of how Amazon does business. The mountains of data that Amazon has, be it from customer behavior on its platform or through digital ads or through AWS, Amazon gets to use this as a free float of sorts to deliver an even better experience. In short, it receives perfect customer feedback all the time, and thanks to user volumes, its competition cannot even hope to match it.

Lastly, there is the one that the Bezos himself creates. As we just mentioned, he presents a great reason to invest in Amazon all by himself. These three moats combined create a pretty unique opportunity for a company in this day and age. Even Google doesn't have the diversity of data that Amazon has.

All in all, Amazon is a no brainer investment for the future and is one that will only grow from here.

THE TRADE DESK

Market cap - $9.74 billion

52 week high/low - 323.78/136

Here we have yet another billion-dollar company that some experts call "the next Netflix." The Trade Desk (TTD) operates in the B2B advertising space, and as such, its business model is likely going to intimidate a few investors. However, the model itself is simpler to understand that it seems on the surface.

TTD is what is called a "buy-side advertising enabler." This means that if you work for an ad agency and are looking to buy advertising space across different forms of media, you can log in to TTD's platform and instantly purchase slots. In the past, given the dominance of television networks, ad buyers used to negotiate with the networks directly.

These days, there are many more ad platforms, and thus, there is a need for a single consolidated platform that allows buyers to buy space and thereby plan their budgets more effectively. The old process used to take time, and this is another benefit of a platform like the one TTD provides.

There are many platforms that do what TTD does; however, the business models are fragmented. What this means is, there is much variation between how these platforms do what they do. TTD positions itself as a platform that is solely focused on the buy-side and does not favor any sell-side network. This helps it avoid any conflict of interest.

After all, favoring a particular seller might result in a poor experience for the buyer and even worse, cost them money. The ad industry has traditionally been a buyer's market thanks to the increasing number of sellers. After all, the number of TV networks grows every day and these days; streaming platforms sell space on their networks as well.

Thus, TTD has positioned itself as a trustworthy name in the industry, and this gives it a significant moat in the minds of buyers. The company divides its operations between two categories, informally speaking. The first is what it calls 'linear TV'. This refers to selling ad space on television channels.

Despite the increasingly bleak prospects that cable TV faces, the fact remains that audience numbers are still high. However, it is a highly inefficient market since advertisers cannot collect data or measure the success of their campaigns to a large extent. After all, how can you measure whether someone saw your ad and decided to buy your product if they saw it on TV?

The second line of business is what TTD calls connected TV or CTV. CTV refers to digital advertising platforms outside of Google and Facebook, which are heavyweights in the industry and handle their buy-side all by themselves. What we mean by this is that both companies allow ad buyers to create their accounts and manage everything themselves after analyzing the mountains of data provided to them.

TTD sells ad space on platforms that are outside of these two tech giants. For example, ad space on Hulu is sold through TTD. A number of other streaming services advertise their space on TTD's platform as well. It is in the CTV space that the company stands to make explosive growth.

Analytics

The modern ad world is vastly different from what it was just a decade ago. Back then, ad agencies mostly focused on the creative side of things and used disciplines such as psychology to drive their ad campaigns. These days, advertising is a matter of data crunching.

Pretty much everything can be tracked and interpreted, and as a result, human psychology can now be quantified. A good example of this is how advertisers run A/B split tests where they test different versions of ad copy to measure what works best. The ad executives don't need to guess what will work anymore; they can measure it.

This has led to increasing demand for data from buying platforms. TTD shines in this regard since it is a fully customizable and open platform. This means users are free to add whatever module they wish and can customize tracking metrics. In contrast, even platforms such as Google and Facebook aren't open or customizable. You're stuck with whatever metrics they provide, and that's it.

The customizable nature of TTD has allowed it to stay ahead of its competition, which provides similar facilities to varying degrees. Add this analytical ability to the growing relevance of CTV advertising, and it becomes obvious that TTD is well-positioned to take over a still-nascent market that is growing exponentially. The CEO of TTD, Jeff Green, had this to say recently about the nature of the ad buying industry (Zafar, 2020):

"...the TV ecosystem today, we think of as a little bit of a ticking time bomb...in traditional TV...the users are going away, the number of people watching is declining, but the cost of providing the service has been going up. And the price of the ads has been going up, even though fewer people are watching...so that's making it...less effective on a per-dollar basis than it has been."

This proves that the company is headed in the right direction by ramping up its focus on analytics and customization.

Another aspect of buying patterns that the ad industry is witnessing is the growing need for automation. This is commonly referred to as programmatic ad buying. Programmatic buying is an algorithm-driven process where advertisers can input their desired criteria, and the algorithm goes ahead and bids and buys whatever space is available. This creates greater efficiency in the process since the algorithm can assess which space offers the greatest cost to benefit ratio.

The increased use of analytics in the ad industry has led to buyers becoming ever more cost-conscious, and programmatic ad buying is at the forefront of their needs. A data-driven platform, such as the one TTD provides is necessary for advertisers to tweak their automated ad buys and create greater efficiency in their bidding process.

International Presence

A neglected fact of digital advertising is that many countries in the world are lagging behind the technologically mature markets in terms of infrastructure available and analytics spend. This presents huge opportunities for companies such as TTD to expand their reach.

Having access to data in more sophisticated markets will allow buyers in less developed ones to place more intelligent buys. Think of it this way: If you've ever tried to advertise on Facebook, you will have noticed that the cost of acquiring an American customer is far greater than acquiring one in Denmark.

This is because there is far less competition in the Danish market, and as a result, you receive more bang for your buck. If you cut your teeth in the American market, dominating the Danish space will be easier. This is pretty much what TTD allows advertisers to do by providing them with relevant data measuring capabilities.

In particular, the company plans on expanding in China and Indonesia, where it believes massive growth potential exists. This is something that no other competitor has managed to pull off and TTD's growing presence in the traditionally sealed off Chinese advertising market is cause for optimism for investors.

Client Concentration

TTDs clients are spread out across the board and no single client represents more than 10% of revenues. Two clients currently represent more than 10% of total billings, and this number is down from three in 2018. What's more, the company has a client retention rate of 95% over three years from 2017. This is a great sign since the more diversified a company's client base is, the less it depends on one customer to generate revenues.

Risks

There are a few risks that investors must make a note of when it comes to TTD. The business is a highly technical one, and as such, all tech-driven businesses are open to disruption. TTD is no different in this regard. It is operating in a space that is still immature (programmatic buying), and this market will evolve in ways that management cannot always predict.

The other thing to keep in mind is that TTD is a relatively immature company compared to the other recommendations in this list. It is operating in a highly competitive market, and any loss of technological ability will result in it losing its moat extremely quickly.

Then there's the fact that some of TTD's competitors such as Google's marketing platform and Verizon Media have better resources than them and could decide to enter the space and introduce more innovation at a rapid pace, which TTD cannot handle. Alternatively, it also means that TTD could be the target of an acquisition. This is not a negative, to be clear. Acquiring TTD would be a smart move on the part of a large competitor at this point, and shareholders will likely see significant gains if this happens to pass.

As such, keeping these risks in mind is prudent, and none of them dampen the case for investment in TTD. The stock is set to skyrocket and is a growth stock in every sense of the term.

KEYSIGHT TECHNOLOGIES

Market cap - $17.34 billion

52 week high/low - 110.00/71.03

Keysight is one of those companies that is integral to almost every single company out there. This is because it is a manufacturer and supplier of 5G chips.

It also makes software that is used in every industry from aerospace, auto manufacturing to defense. The primary investment thesis of investing in Keysight is the same as the lesson that was learned back during the gold rush.

The gold rush inspired tons of people to move out West to seek their fortune in desperate little mining towns in the middle of nowhere. The odds of the prospectors being successful was low thanks to the large competition that faced them. Enough movies have been made about what these men went through.

What is not mentioned, is that there were people who became extremely rich off the gold rush. It wasn't the prospectors but the saloons and prospecting equipment sellers. In other words, during the gold rush, the only people who became rich were the ones who sold shovels and booze. This thesis of investing has been reliable throughout the course of history and is the basis for our 2nd and 3rd order consequences cornerstone.

Instead of investing in a hot niche that is crowded with competition, it's far better to invest in companies that are suppliers to the hot niche. The supplier is sure to benefit from the huge demand that will flow to them thanks to the number of companies in that niche.

A good example of this thesis are companies such as Keysight and Intel. These companies don't manufacture the finished products but make products that are integral to those finished goods. Every electronic item out there needs a chip. While Intel focuses on producing chips for computers and smartphones, Keysight focuses on chips for industrial purposes.

This is what has led the company to establish a broad customer base, and this is unlikely to change. The niche that Keysight operates in has high barriers to entry thanks to its being a hugely technical field. Furthermore, the established nature of Keysight's business means that competition is unlikely to win over too many of Keysight's clientele.

The company began life as a subsidiary of Hewlett Packard and was spun off in 2012. Thus, while its life as a public company is short, its expertise stretches a long way back. This is what has enabled it to grow spectacularly since its formation, and it has avoided the usual hiccups that new companies face.

Keysight's business is grouped into three different categories. The first is the communication solutions group and this group serves the aerospace, dense, and government industries. One of the key drivers of growth here is the rise of 5G, as well as the growing complexity of semiconductor devices as automation grows. The group's products find their way into products that are used for communication, satellites, radar, and surveillance systems. This group raked in $715 million in profits during the previous year.

The second division is the electronic industrial solutions group, and the profits for this group come in at $294 million. The group's focus is on consumer technology, and in this regard, the group designs software and testing solutions. This software has a major role to play in the validation, optimization, installation, and manufacturing of consumer products.

Manufacturers of computers, computer peripherals, consumer electronics, OEM products, medical equipment are the group's primary customers. Given the broader breadth, this group typically sells more units and is less specialized than the communications group.

Lastly, we have Keysight's Ixia solutions group that is responsible for $29 million in profits. This group focuses on testing the security of virtual networks and their associated components and applications. This means the group is involved in producing software to secure a company's hardware, software and other services. The group's primary income is derived from installation and warranty contracts.

Growth

It's easy to forget that Keysight is still a growing company despite its size. A lot of its existing business stems from when the company was a division within HP, and the company has begun implementing its own sales channels effectively. The results of this have been phenomenal.

The last three quarters of 2019 witnessed huge growth and all quarters resulted in the company earning far in excess of analyst estimates. As a result, share prices have become a bit inflated but they still remain a bargain over the course of the long term.

As of this writing, 78 of the Fortune 100 companies are clients of Keysight. The business the company is going to source from them is only going to grow thanks to the ever-increasing demand on processor chips that the internet of things is going to require.

The upcoming decade is going to witness the birth of self-driving cars and increasingly smart devices. All of this will only accelerate demand, and Keysight is well-positioned to handle all of this. The research firm Gartner estimates that by 2022, the average American home will contain 22 smart devices.

The defense industry is also another sector that is going to witness increased demand for Keysight's products. The massive human toll of warfare has led to a push to create robots that have greater involvement in combat, and these will need sophisticated technological inputs.

Overall, Keysight is in a great position to serve all of these increased demands.

Software

Despite the firm's focus on hardware, it is the Ixia solutions group where the most investment is taking place. This is because as time moves forward, implementing software as a solution (SaaS) revenue streams will become of primary importance. After all, hardware needs to be installed only once, but the software requires regular maintenance and upgrades.

At some point, Keysight will be called upon to maintain the hardware it installs, and this is why the shift in investment to SaaS is a good sign. The best part of this business model is the relatively high margins it generates. All of this is an excellent sign for the company moving forward.

Customer Base

The customer base of Keysight is varied, and the best part of this is that not a single company accounts for more than five percent of the overall business. This means that the company is not overly exposed to natural disasters such as the COVID-19 crisis. Evidence of this can be seen in the performance of the stock. Which has held up far better than its peers thus far.

This being said, some risks are present for Keysight. The highly technical nature of the business means that significant cash needs to be spent on R&D. As we mentioned earlier, America is behind China when it comes to the adoption and development of 5G technology.

The defense sector will especially place a huge demand on Keysight for these products, and if they don't happen to be up to scratch, the prospect of losing a key customer looms. It also opens the door for an upstart competitor to enter the market. Despite this risk, the pedigree of management, as well as their track record, indicates that the company should be able to handle this well.

The recession that will most probably follow the viral outbreak should pose no threat to the company. It has a strong balance sheet and is secure in terms of cash and financing options. Continued investment into research and development is the key to growth and executives seem to understand this basic fact pretty well. The switch to SaaS and software-centric business models also indicate that they are on top of the changing economics of the industry.

Chinese Exposure

Given the technologically sensitive nature of their business, Keysight has almost no Chinese exposure. It does source a few parts from that country, but all in all, the lockdowns have had no effect on Keysight's business.

Competition from Chinese OEMs is what threatens Keysight's domination in overseas markets where buyers are not as keen to buy American. The challenge here will be for the company to maintain its dominance in the face of an increasingly aggressive Chinese supply in the 5G and related technological space.

There are mitigating factors here, though. While the consumer-facing business lines will be impacted by the threat of Chinese products, the governmental business operations, and other high tech operations are unlikely to be affected for now. It remains to be seen how Chinese firms such as Huawei pivot from manufacturing low-level consumer-centric 5G goods to more complex hardware solutions.

For now, though, Keysight is ahead of its competitors and is a great investment. It has stable management that has a clear succession plan in place and has a history of stable earnings growth. Its customer base is extremely varied, and Keysight produces the one thing that all of them need no matter what. This ensures a steady demand.

All in all, the company is well poised to grow its profits well beyond the next decade.

COCA-COLA

Market cap - $210.38 billion

52 week high/low - 60.13/36.27

Coca-Cola needs no introduction. Everyone has heard of it, and everyone has drunk the beverage at some point in their lives. The company has been a financial giant of America with an increasing dividend for 57 years in a row. This makes it a dividend aristocrat with astonishing ease.

The company itself has always been viewed as a steady earner in times of distress and has always rewarded long term investors. Coca-Cola stock has never been an exciting headline grabber, but its real returns come from its steady dividend as well as the fact that it tends to outperform markets during downtrends, even if it lags during uptrends.

A huge seal of approval as far as the investment worthiness of the company is the fact that Coca-Cola remains one of Berkshire Hathaway's largest holdings, with Cherry Coca-Cola being the chairman's beverage of choice. This endorsement notwithstanding, Coca-Cola has been facing some headwinds in the past decade.

The world keeps changing, and consumer preferences change along with it. It began with firearms and tobacco companies being attacked in the mainstream and having vigorous campaigns mounted against them. We're not here to judge the moral relevance of these campaigns but are merely tracing a trend factually. Advertising bans soon arrived, and these days, while tobacco companies are profitable and steady earners, they have lost the ability to grow explosively.

The same trend is catching on when it comes to the fast food and soft drinks sector. Companies that own their assets, such as McDonald's, are good bets when it comes to the ability to thrive during such times. With soft drinks, the challenges are different. There are no real estate assets the company can own. After all, no one goes to a sit-down restaurant just to drink Coca-Cola.

Instead, the focus ought to be on reducing overhead expenses and diversifying away from a single product line. While health consciousness will reduce the demand for Coca-Cola over the upcoming years like never before, this doesn't mean that the company has to sell bottles of Coca-Cola to remain profitable.

Coca-Cola has taken several steps in this regard, and these form the primary reason as to why it is a great investment.

Reduced Overhead

Coca-Cola is one of the best-structured businesses on the planet. While people think of it as a soft drinks company, the fact is that in business terms, Coca-Cola is a beverage distributor. It has always separated its distribution business from its direct to consumer bottling business.

The company owned a number of bottling plants around the world and in the United States, but the revenues from bottling were separate from the revenues earned via syrup distribution. This decision was a far-sighted one and is paying off now. Given the headwinds Coca-Cola faces, it has begun divesting its bottling plants and is increasingly shifting towards becoming a syrup distributor.

This reduces overhead massively since bottling plants are factories that require massive capital investment and maintenance. A syrup distributor, on the other hand, has to simply manufacture the mix and sell it to the bottlers. The infrastructure required to make syrup is far smaller than what it takes to bottle the finished product.

For starters, bottles aren't needed. The syrup is transferred in refrigerated trucks and is stored in plastic bags within cardboard boxes. All of this reduces overhead massively. Which indicates that Coca-Cola has read the signs and is restructuring its business to meet the challenge.

Its operating margin now stands at 29% as a result; this is unheard of for a company of its size.

Diversification

Coca-Cola has long favored diversifying beyond its Coca-Cola syrup product offering. The company owns a number of brands around the world that have significant market share in their own right. Here is a list of brands the Coca-Cola owns:

- Sprite (soft drink)
- Fanta (soft drink)
- Schweppes (soda water)
- Appletiser (sparkling juice)
- Dasani (mineral water)
- Powerade (sports drink)
- SmartWater (mineral water)
- Vitaminwater (sports drink)
- ZICO (sports drink)
- Minute Maid (juice)
- innocent (juice)
- Simply (juice)
- fairlife (dairy)
- AdeS (assorted beverages)

- Costa Coffee (coffee chain)
- Georgia Coffee (coffee chain)

This isn't the full list, but as you can see, there are a number of brands in here that are heavyweights in their own right. All of this means that Coca-Cola as a company, still has a lot of demand beyond sugary drinks.

Growth

Tagging a company of this size with the 'growth' label might seem ridiculous, but the fact is that Coca-Cola has a long way to grow at the moment. Brands within the Coca-Cola family such as Diet Coca-Cola, Coca-Cola Zero, and Coca-Cola Vanilla and so on have a smaller footprint than the primary product.

Investors often confuse the American market as being representative for the rest of the world, but this is not the case. Internationally, classic Coca-Cola is still the bestseller, but the company has only begun to market and push the other lines of Coca-Cola. For example, five years ago it was close to impossible to find Diet Coca-Cola in India, but now, the country consumes the drink in massive quantities.

Add to this the fact that there are other product lines that the company can push. For example, Dasani water isn't widely available outside America at the moment, but the company is actively pushing the product, and there is massive potential for sales to increase.

Moat

When it comes to Coca-Cola it is impossible to ignore the sheer size of its moat. The name 'Coca-Cola' is widely recognized to the extent that it is used to talk about other types of products as well. Everyone and their grandma has consumed the product, and the color and font of the Coca-Cola script are widely recognized.

Then there's the longevity that the company has displayed. It has been around forever and has weathered six recessions in the United States alone. It has expanded into countries that have come to associate Coca-Cola with America and stand as a symbol of refreshment and a lot more around the world.

It is fashionable to make statements that imply that a giant is about to fall but, to be honest, such statements tend to be false for the most part. It takes a lot of work for a mainstay of the American economy to fall apart, and as of now, this day seems very far away for Coca-Cola. As of this writing, there are less than five countries around the world where Coca-Cola isn't the top selling soft drink.

Risks

As with everything, there are risks to investing in Coca-Cola. The company has been investing in creating further product lines and diversifying its product portfolio. It has expanded into snacks as well. All of this is a clear sign that it is witnessing a decrease in demand for the core product.

This might seem like bad news, it is, to a certain extent, but it can be mitigated with good diversification. It remains to be seen how well the management carries this out. It is a significant challenge the company faces. Replacing income that will be reduced from the Coca-Cola lines is a stiff task.

Due to these developments, the company's balance sheet has become more lever- aged. Currently, the debt to equity ratio stands at 0.71. Debt stands for the sum of all the loans and liabilities the company has. Equity is the capital it has in the form of shareholder value and represents the amount of a company shareholders own. This is despite divesting a large number of its bottling plants. In compari- son, the debt to equity in 2010 stood at 0.1.

What's more, Coca-Cola is increasing the level of debt it will carry by issuing bonds worth $5 billion with maturities ranging from 7, 10, 20, and 30 years respectively. This will increase the burden of interest expense it has to carry. Currently, interest expense is 2.7% of revenues, which is still manageable, given the fact that Coca-Cola doesn't carry too many capital heavy assets.

The case for Coca-Cola mostly comes down to this: The expertise of manage- ment and their ability to diversify and evolve the core business. There is no denying that demand for the core Coca-Cola products will be lower 30 years from now. However, Coca-Cola has already diversified to such an extent that it isn't solely dependent on the core drink line as it was 20 years ago.

As such, this means that the company has been anticipating a slowdown in demand for a long time. Which explains the re-structuring of the company to meet these changing conditions well in advance. Then there's the fact that almost none of its product lines are likely to witness a drop in demand no matter how tough the economic outlook gets. Be it a recession or a boom, soft drink consumption will remain steady, and as the biggest bully in the space, Coca-Cola is unlikely to go anywhere but up.

ZOOM COMMUNICATIONS

Market cap - $40.41 billion

52 week high/low - 181.50/59.94

This company has become one of the coronavirus darlings and is one of the few companies that have benefited from the pandemic. If you weren't acquainted with the software before, you sure are now. However, popularity alone doesn't make for a great investment thesis. A good example of this are marijuana stocks that have been the rage since legalization. A large number of those stocks are now exploring new lows.

Zoom has long been a great investment. Since its IPO in 2019, where it debuted at $61 per share, the company has managed to grow despite a tough market. Tough in this context describes the conditions that were facing cloud computing companies. Many stocks in this sector saw selloffs of over 30%. However, Zoom managed to rise above its IPO price which was impressive.

The company has also been one of those rare Silicon Valley unicorns that managed to make money before going public. As of 2019, the company's total revenue grew to $622.7 million, which represents an 88% increase from 2018.

However if you note the market cap number listed above, you will notice that the valuation of the company is ludicrously high, based on current numbers. There's no denying that Zoom fits the qualities of a stock that you should ignore if you were to follow our previously listed principles. It is a media darling at the moment. Which means everyone is piling into it because they've heard the name, and have experienced the platform to an increasing degree thanks to the pandemic.

This has led to Zoom selling at a ridiculous 50x multiple to sales and an even more ridiculous valuation when it comes to the earnings ratio. A lot of sensible investors will be scared away by these multiples and they would be justified in doing so. So, why are we recommending Zoom as an investment?

For starters, there's the product itself. The software was popular even before the pandemic thanks to its sleek interface and ease of use. Now that active users have grown to 12.92 million on a monthly basis, the software is all set to become even more popular. A large part of Zoom's rapid growth in its user base has to do with its product-market fit.

Tech analysts often use this term to describe the 'X factor' that a particular stock or company has. They use this to explain why a product achieves virality. As such, no one knows what this really means, and it's one of those terms that are a catch-all for inexplicable behavior. Much like how market selloff in the 90s and in the previous decade was due to Arabs selling stuff, "product market fit" is a catch-all term for viral phenomena.

One of the key reasons for Zoom's growth that we can easily discern is that it does not need any account-based dependency across platforms. This means you could be working on MS Outlook and still use it. Other collaboration software such as Skype and Google Hangouts are either clunky or require authentication from multiple accounts before logging in.

This played a key role in the early adoption of Zoom. Most importantly, growth was driven from the ground up. Meaning, it wasn't imposed on workers by management. Instead, it was lower-level employees who insisted that management use the software. All of this bodes well for long term user retention. With telecommuting on the rise and set to become the norm over the next decade, Zoom is right where it wants to be.

Future Prospects

As we mentioned earlier, the earnings multiples on Zoom stocks are nonsensical. The company is selling close to 260X projected earnings, which is extremely high even for a darling tech stock. Compare this with a multiple of 130X for Shopify and Slack, and you'll see how overvalued Zoom currently is.

Despite this, Zoom has excellent long term growth prospects. The market size of communications as a service has been estimated to be $43 billion (Mckenna, 2020). Zoom's position as a leader in this space and its current valuation means that there is a long way to go.

What's more, Zoom is in the process of releasing a new feature called Zoom Phone which is VoIP calling without the need for video. As of current writing, 16% of the total workforce in the United States telecommutes. This was before the virus hit, and it doesn't include American workers traveling overseas or the large gig economy that exists in the form of freelancers and consultants.

All of these numbers are set not just to increase, but explode. What's more, this doesn't take into account the international market where Zoom has witnessed huge growth. From 2018-2020, Zoom sourced 17-20% of its total revenues from EMEA regions as well as Asia-Pacific countries.

Another great quality that Zoom has consistently displayed is its ability to convert free users into paid customers. A lot of SaaS companies rely on the Freemium model of business. The Freemium model means they offer basic features on a free basis but more advanced features for a fee. A high conversion rate indicates that the premium features add significant value, and this is a great sign for sustainable growth. Many SaaS companies fall victim to free users driving up operating costs, and not being able to offset set that with the required number of paid users. Zoom does not have these issues.

Problems

Despite all of the positives that we've highlighted, the fact remains that Zoom is still an extremely young company, and there are many risks it faces. Despite the growth in users during this time, it still faces the challenge of having to retain those users. Tech apps are extremely prone to having their users flee to some other platform at the drop of a hat.

Remember when Skype was all the rage? It existed back when apps were still called programs! You would reason that backing from a huge company such as Microsoft would do it a world of good, but this hasn't really been the case. The software is often mentioned as an also-ran at this point.

Zoom is susceptible to these risks as well, so user growth alone won't cut it. The primary feature that drew people to the app was the ease of use and the ability to work across platforms. While the consumer usage is what is making headlines of late, it is the business usage that drives the business. How Zoom handles the surge of users remains to be seen.

As of now, the signs are promising. Zoom recently made news when it was sued by a developer out in California, claiming that the company had shared his data without his consent. Soon, news websites were flooded with headlines stating that Zoom was unreliable and that it wasn't end-to-end encrypted. A lot of this was hysteria, so it's worth delving deeper into this and understanding what really happened.

First, let's deal with the case that brought all of this to light. The developer's claim was primarily that the company had shared his data without proper notice. Zoom responded in a blog post by saying that the issue had occurred due to them installing a Facebook software development kit, which allowed users to login using their Facebook Id.

As a result, Facebook collected information about the users logging in and stored it on its platform. As such, it was Facebook that was at fault, and Zoom's mistake was not to know that this was possible, which is sloppy. However, the company owned up to this mistake in a blog post and stated the following (Yuan, 2020):

'We originally implemented the "Login with Facebook" feature using the Facebook SDK for iOS (Software Development Kit) in order to provide our users with another convenient way to access our platform. However, we were made aware on Wednesday, March 25, 2020, that the Facebook SDK was collecting device information unnecessary for us to provide our services. The information collected by the Facebook SDK did not include information and activities related to meetings such as attendees, names, notes, etc., but rather included information about devices such as the mobile OS type and version, the device time zone, device OS, device model and carrier, screen size, processor cores, and disk space'

Following this, further investigations were conducted, and this is when the lack of end to end encryption came to light. Initial reporting suggested that Zoom had marketed their software as having this level of encryption, but it looked like they had lied. This is untrue.

The issue lay with the way the encryption keys were being stored. The data itself is fully encrypted, and it is impossible for Zoom or anyone else to access. However, the keys that unlock the data were being stored by Zoom in its own cloud. The reason it was doing so was this: Zoom was originally designed for business use.

Business users typically place additional security measures across their networks prior to logging in and this ensures that encryption keys are stored on their own servers. The sudden rise in consumer usage meant that Zoom had to begin storing keys on its own cloud since there was nowhere else for them to store it. The sudden and massive rise in user numbers is what caused the issue, and there wasn't malice on the company's part.

The CEO of Zoom, Eric Yuan described it in a blog post. He stated that the product was designed to be used by large corporate users who carry out their own separate security checks on their networks. As a result, Zoom didn't need to carry a lot of protocols that are required for daily consumer use.

The rapid and unprecedented growth of the user base didn't leave the company with enough time to build these features, and as a result, Zoom was caught off guard.

All in all, the company had issues and dealt with everything in a transparent manner and didn't lie to its users or cover up its efforts, like how Facebook and Google have done in the past. This is a sign of competent management that understands the current climate surrounding data privacy and takes it seriously.

As far as management indicators go, these are pretty strong ones. This didn't stop the negative headlines from rolling in. Media darling Elon Musk banned Zoom usage across Tesla while in what was effectively a candid admission of an inferior product, direct rival Google banned the usage of Zoom as well. The implication here is that Google's own employees preferred Zoom to Hangouts.

All in all, Zoom is not without risk, but the ability of management to weather this crisis and display transparency is something that bodes well for its future. We would like to see Zoom trade at lower prices, and you'll learn why after using our company valuation tool in the next chapter.

TELADOC HEALTH

Market cap - $11.25 billion

52 week high/low - 176.40/48.57

With everything becoming digital these days, it stands to reason that healthcare would follow in these footsteps as well. The global telehealth market is projected to reach a size of $55.6 billion by 2025, and Teladoc is at the forefront of this revolution. In-person visitation has lagged behind the rest of the healthcare segment thus far in terms of digital applications.

After all, it is tough to diagnose someone without seeing them in person. The outbreak of COVID-19 has changed this space completely. With increased risks associated with in-person contact, video conferencing ability, and e-consultations are on the rise. While you might be tempted to think that this is just a virus related fad, the numbers say otherwise.

Teladoc has witnessed huge growth over the past decade. In fact, in the field of telehealth services the company is far ahead of giants of the space such as Humana and UnitedHealth Group. It also happens to be the only telehealth service provider that trades publicly, which puts it far ahead of its competition.

Furthermore, the viral outbreak had opened people's eyes as to how effective virtual doctor visits can be. An initial analysis suggests that this behavior will continue in the future as people become more secure with this form of doctor consultation. Overall, telehealth and telemedicine is a "mega trend" that is bound to become even more popular over the coming decades, and Teladoc is right at the forefront of it.

The company currently covers treatment for a variety of medical issues. As of 2019, Teladoc provides virtual consultation services for over 450 medical subspecialties. These also cover mental health services through its subsidiary BetterHelp.

Within the United States, the company has over 36.7 million unique users (up 61% YoY) who are paid members and 19.3 million users (up 104% YoY) who pay one-time visit fees on the platform. Thanks to the acquisition of Advance Medical Healthcare Management Services, the company now provides services in 130 countries and in 30 languages 24 hours a day.

Acquisitions are the primary mode of growth for Teladoc. In addition to patient-facing services, the company also invests in developing enterprise platforms for hospitals and physicians to bring them on board its network. Nine out of 10 insurance providers are supported on the platform, and this has ensured broad appeal.

B2B

Teladoc currently provides B2B healthcare solutions to over 12,000 businesses across America, with 40% of these businesses being Fortune 500 companies. The company has also partnered with CVS pharmacy to position itself as the virtual healthcare service provider of choice. In addition to this, Teladoc works with 50 major American health insurers and over 70 international health insurers and finance firms.

The CVS partnership, titled MinuteClinic expanded from 18 to 26 states last year. The revenue model is pretty simple. Clients pay a monthly subscription fee, and there are no hidden fees within this.

The real driver of growth in the B2B segment has been the adoption of multiple services by clients already on the platform. Teladoc states that 40% of existing clients subscribe to two or more services within its network with BetterHelp witnessing the largest growth.

TECHNICAL ABILITIES

A significant advantage that Teladoc has is that it can collect usage data and analytics about the users and physicians on its platform. The company has strict data protection policies, so patients do not need to worry about medical histories being leaked. The analytics that the company collects are primarily designed to develop better engagement with existing users as well as to drive growth by signing up new users.

These analytics are what fuel the company's marketing strategy, and thus far, all campaigns have been a success with new user signups increasing at a record pace. The company's platform itself has been designed, so that introduction of new services is seamless.

This happens due to deep investment in infrastructure that allows Teladoc not only to provide a robust platform but also allows for real-time eligibility checking and integration with insurance companies.

Research

There are many roadblocks that telehealth companies need to navigate as of this writing. First off, many of the treatments for complex or severe conditions cannot be prescribed without an in-person visit. This is understandable and is something that telehealth providers will not overcome anytime soon.

A bigger hurdle that can be overcome is the ability of doctors to prescribe treatments virtually. To this effect, Teladoc has partnered with Thomas Jefferson University to offer a fellowship aimed at training doctors in virtual care. The company has also teamed up with the University of Southern California to research antibiotic prescription in virtual healthcare.

These efforts prove that Teladoc takes its commitment to its business seriously. They have been in business for over 10 years and have been steadily expanding in a growing industry. While it has been gaining attention thanks to the COVID-19 outbreak, the company is more than just a short term fad.

There is a lot going to Teladoc. It is a relatively mature company operating in a fast-growing field. It has ample cash reserves and doesn't have many competitors in sight. The fact that it is far ahead of the curve of its much bigger rivals in the space means that if its upward curve continues, it should be a prime takeover candidate which will ensure investors receive some pretty sizable gains.

LULULEMON ATHLETICA

Market cap - $25.94 billion

52 week high/low - 266.20/128.85

Another trend that has been growing is holistic fitness. While the previous decade saw the expansion of gyms and fitness clubs, this decade has seen the growth of fitness routines such as calisthenics and yoga.

The thing with such routines is that they're a lifestyle as well as a training regimen. They inspire extreme loyalty amongst those who practice them, and this royalty extends to any brands that serve this space. One of the biggest companies that inspire such cult-like loyalty is Lululemon Athletica.

From the outside looking in, Lululemon sells a bunch of overpriced clothes along with mats and other accessories that seem to make no sense. For instance, one of its products happens to be a yoga mat that is priced at $88 and headbands for women that are priced at $40. These prices don't make much sense to the outsider, but to someone who lives the lifestyle, they're perfectly fine. It's the same phenomenon as with Starbucks' prices. Lululemon Inspires extremely high levels of loyalty, and purchasing its products is a bit like buying your way into a club of fellow lifestyle seekers.

The majority of the brand's customers are women. Which makes sense since, in North America, the majority of yoga and alternative fitness practitioners happen to be women. Lululemon's apparel and accessories are hot sellers but they also stand up to scrutiny in terms of quality. Unlike apparel from other fitness brands, the clothes are not produced in sweatshops in third world countries, and this is often something that appeals to shoppers.

Scarcity and Growth

One of the things that Lululemon has going for it is the fact that for a brand that inspires so much loyalty, the number of physical outlets it has is laughably low. The brand had just 38 physical stores around the world till the end of 2018 and by the end of 2019, had opened an additional 51 stores.

Obviously, in hindsight, this seems like a bad investment, and no doubt it will hurt during the short term. Given that yoga studios and fitness centers of all kinds have closed, the brand is likely to witness a few tough quarters this year. However, a lot depends on when isolation protocols will ease. If we witness restrictions ease before the holiday season this year, sales could increase and power profits.

However, all of that is conjecture. As of now, we can conclude that the low number of physical outlets contributes to creating low overhead costs as well as creates a scarcity effect. The fact that its stores are located mostly in trendy cities only adds to its allure. All in all, Lululemon does a great job of marketing its lifestyle-based message instead of pushing itself as just an apparel manufacturer.

This allows it to differentiate itself from the other giants in the space such as Nike, Adidas, and Puma.

Niche

The company is based out of Canada but counts the United States as its biggest market. Over 90% of its customers are based in the US. A good way to think of its appeal is to liken it to Starbucks. It is a place that offers luxury at affordable prices, even if it isn't the cheapest.

Its customers recognize all of this and see it as an indispensable part of their lifestyle. Then there's the fact the company was perhaps the first fitness apparel maker that dedicated itself to creating clothes for women. The founder of Lululemon, Chip Wilson, (we'll deal with him in more detail shortly) mentions the practice of 'shrink it and pink it' that was relevant in the fitness apparel industry at the time (Lieber, 2018)

This refers to shrinking the size of men's fitness apparel and coloring it pink, thereby creating women's apparel. Women noticed this needless to say and had to resort to wearing dance leggings that were simply not made for exercise routines such as Yoga. Wilson's solutions to redesign apparel created a splash, and this is what helped develop the cult-like obsession that its customers have.

There is a roaring second market for used Lululemon clothing. Luxury brands such as Chanel and Gucci often witness huge interest in used goods of theirs but Lululemon is the only athletic apparel manufacturer that draws such interest. Scarcity is at the heart of this once again. It begins with the way each style is introduced into the market.

Garments are given names that signify their uniqueness as well as their color. Next, the company gives purchasers just 14 days to return goods they're unhappy with. This is a far stricter return policy than what most retailers practice, and it does leave them with unhappy customers. However, it creates supply for the secondary market.

Lastly, Lululemon produces fixed quantities of its styles and never replenishes stocks. This means that if you own a pair of leggings, you're one of the few people in the world that do. The scarcity model is even enforced geographically. Styles that are released in say, Tokyo, are not released in New York.

This has led to blogs and communities being set up that follow Lululemon's style releases with a fervor that is usually reserved for fashion week luxury brands. Lululemon is well aware of these practices and has gone so far as to deny service to suspected resellers. During certain periods, it bars people from buying more than a certain number of items of clothing to stop them from reselling it at a higher markup (Lieber, 2015).

Events the company holds, such as the Sea Breeze Half Marathon, tend to witness huge sales of items that immediately pop up on eBay and other reseller sites. While the company discourages these practices, from an investor's perspective, all of this screams economic moat.

Diversification

Lululemon has long since recognized its brand power and has invested in a tech startup named Mirror. This company aims to develop smart mirrors that can be used to provide fitness instruction along with further recommendations. It's not hard to see how this could help Lululemon expand its product offerings.

While its retail outlets are small in number, Lululemon's website is a huge driver of sales, as are its special events that are regular fan fests. While physical stores will naturally be closed right now, the high level of loyalty, the brand inspires will only boost online sales and will help it diversify its revenue streams well into the future.

Management

This is going to be perhaps the most soap-operatic portion of this book. While the founder of Lululemon, Chip Wilson, is rightly credited as being one of the retail industry's visionaries. The company he created refuses even to acknowledge him on their 'about us' page. A major reason for this is the drama that Wilson created while he was in charge of the company.

Never one to hold back on his views, he said he created Lululemon primarily to help women "make their butts look better" and one of his self-confessed metrics for this was the number of compliments men would give women without realizing exactly why the woman's butt looked better than before (Lieber, 2018).

One of his more famous policies was to hire employees who were family-oriented and wanted to have children in the future. He even went as far as to dub kids as being "nature's orgasm." None of this pleased shareholders, but there's no denying it did create an aura of rebellion around the company and helped it achieve a cult-like following.

Speaking of cults, Wilson is also credited with developing the self-help employee training program that all recruits go through when they join the company. The

141

details are far too bizarre to recount here, and you can refer to the sources at the end of this book for a full account.

Despite all of his faults, Wilson also ended up designing perhaps what is one of the best protocols for on-floor sales techniques. Lululemon's salespeople are instructed to adhere to a very specific sales manner. If the customer stares at a product for six seconds (yes, it's timed), the salesperson (called an "educator") has to deliver an enthusiastic speech about how wonderful the product is. At this point, if the customer doesn't have further questions, the salesperson walks away.

They return when the customer stares at another product for six seconds and the same routine begins all over again. This sounds strange, to say the least, but it has resulted in Lululemon achieving per square foot sales numbers on par with Tiffany's and Apple, both of whom sell vastly more expensive products.

Wilson is long gone from the company, having been ousted acrimoniously in 2013, and the management that is in place now is far better suited to run a large public corporation. While Wilson was best suited for the company's buccaneering days, Lululemon is a giant now and isn't really an underdog. As such, his presence would only destabilize the brand's position.

Financial Position

It isn't all just cults and spandex when it comes to Lululemon. The company has an astonishing $1 billion in cash and has close to zero debt. This is pretty remarkable for a retailer that has just opened 51 new stores. As a result, the management does not foresee the need to have to borrow money via debt offerings or equity financing.

What's more, the company has been buying back its stock throughout 2019 and will probably continue to do so, provided sales don't fall off a cliff completely in 2020. Despite the headwinds facing the company and the female-centric sales material, men's apparel saw a jump of 34% along with the operating margin increasing as well. Based on current numbers, projected growth and unique marketplace positioning, the company is in a good financial position to deal with the current crisis and is well set for the future.

BAIDU

Market cap - $34.02 billion

52 week high/low - 186.22/82.00

As we've already outlined before, China has made the leap over the past decade from a growing economy to emerge as a truly dominant world power. The country seems to be shedding the last few characteristics of a 'growing economy' and is now a fully grown one, even if the immediate effects of this are not being felt.

One of the major reasons for this is the nature of the government, and the way it controls the spread of information. Transparency is extremely low in China, and investors are wary, correctly so, of investing in any Chinese company. While the likes of Alibaba prove that fully private enterprises can flourish, the fact is that it is far easier to grow in China when you have strong government ties.

Political leanings aside, this means that any investment in China is better off if it is done in a company that has good ties to the government and is in a critical area of growth. Chinese government is focusing its efforts on developing its technology. The country is seeking to move away from its image as a manufacturer of cheap toys and goods. Instead moving into the high tech space.

The rise of Huawei, a firm that was founded by a former high ranking Chinese soldier, in the 5G space is proof of this. All tech stocks receive patronage from the government, and Baidu is one of the beneficiaries of this. The company is virtually unheard of outside of China but within the country and in parts of SE Asia, it trounces Google completely.

Baidu is one of the largest search engines on the planet thanks to the volume of its users. Google is officially banned in China thanks to censorship issues, and this gives Baidu a near monopoly over the Chinese internet. As of current writing, the platform has over 700 million users. The staggering aspect is that this number represents just half of the Chinese population.

With internet coverage set to grow in China and with the government effectively favoring Baidu's monopoly over the internet and flow of information, the company is almost certainly going to witness an increase in the number of users over the next few decades.

Revenue Model

The business is a replica of Google, and as such Baidu's revenue model is the same. It relies on pay per click (PPC) advertising, and as the largest ad platform in China, its earnings have been rising steadily over the past decade. Recently, PPC revenue dropped thanks to increasing controls of ad standards, but once the dust settles and as advertisers adjust to the new standards, revenues should be back where they were.

Like Google, Baidu has long since moved away from its search engine roots and has become a full-fledged tech company. It is the only company in the world that has received a license to operate self-driving vehicles and currently operates a bus successfully within its campus.

It has also invested heavily in driverless cars, and over the next decade, these are expected to rollout. News is predictably bullish as it is with every Chinese news source, but there are signs that these news items are genuine. While these lines of business are not profitable or even collecting revenue at the moment, they do hold huge promise for the future.

In addition to the vehicles themselves, Baidu has also developed an open-source software named Apollo that can be used to program driverless cars. The business model here is the same as what Google did with the Android phone operating system, and the hope is that as more companies enter the space, Baidu can become the software provider of choice instead of getting into costly hardware investments.

As Google has YouTube, so does Baidu have iQiyi. Here, Baidu faces some pretty stiff competition. The first competitor is Tencent video, which is backed by the giant Tencent, and the second is Youku Tudou, which is owned by Alibaba. These three companies are present in the same space and engage in one form of state-sanctioned competition or another.

It appears that for now, Baidu is not favored in this race with Alibaba leading the way. One reason for this is that its platform is actually an amalgam of two earlier video platforms that were developed late in the previous decade. As a result, the company received an early boost in terms of the user base. However, Baidu's dominance of the search engine world does mean that it can compete with these other platforms even if it cannot dominate.

Ad revenue from the video-sharing platform is lower than PPC ads in search. This has as much to do with Baidu's lack of penetration as it has to do with how unsuitable video platforms are for the PPC model. After all, even YouTube barely makes any money and its ads aren't the most efficient.

iQiyi is much more than just a YouTube clone though. In fact, all of the Chinese video platforms can be seen as a combination of Netflix and YouTube. iQiyi is often dubbed the Netflix of China but this is simply because it's an easy way to explain what the platform is all about. It's a bit more than that as we've just described. It is also an online gaming platform that is a bit like Steam and Twitch where players can subscribe to play games as well as share their in game heroics across the network.

One of the fields that Baidu is spending a lot of money on is AI. Chinese firms have a massive head start on the rest of the world in terms of AI thanks to the surveillance that the government engages in. This gives them access to far more data than is available in other societies. Moral quandaries aside, Baidu is no different in this respect.

It has developed a voice assistant (think Alexa) called DuerOS which seamlessly works on smartphones and other smart devices. It is witnessing huge growth. While the company isn't clear on the user growth, one way of measuring this is via the growth in users of the app. This number grew by 21% over 2019 with previous years recording growth as well.

In addition to this, the number of voice queries on DuerOS grew fivefold to 4.2 billion queries per month. Currently, DuerOS is available on Baidu produced Xiaodu devices which span from speakers to smart displays. In the B2B space, Baidu has an AWS clone in Baidu Cloud which offers server space and IT infrastructure services to enterprises.

The company has a few diversified revenue streams but is still heavily reliant on the effectiveness of its PPC ads. In this regard, it is similar to Google, but like Google, the plan is to ramp up earnings from other areas of the business as technology continues to mature.

Performance

A major knock against Baidu is that its stock performance has been abysmal over 2019 and this was before the virus hit. However, this is just a reflection of the emotion driven selloff that afflicted its sector.

A big reason for the terrible performance was that all Chinese tech stocks were overvalued to begin with. The increasing growth and prominence of China as a technological hub prompted many investors to move into Chinese companies and tech were recipients of this money.

As a result, valuation levels grew to absurd levels. Consider that the stock is now selling at a 14x earnings multiple. For comparison's sake, Google is selling at 24x. This shows how grossly undervalued Baidu currently is and how the impact of the virus has been mispriced.

While it is true that a recession will impact Baidu's earnings, just how bad will the impact be on its core business? With physical stores shutting down, businesses will be forced to turn online. This leaves Baidu as the only viable outlet for advertising, and it already dominates 80% of the sector.

Thus, the domination is likely going to be extended moving forward. Over the short term, the company is addressing its cash needs by issuing debt to the tune of $1 billion in short term notes. This should see it tide over any recession concerns.

The Chinese government has been moving swiftly to contain the impact of the virus within the country. All of this means that the Chinese economy is likely to bounce back faster than the rest of the world, and as a result, Baidu's prospects will behave the same way. All in all, Baidu might be a bit more opaque than other Western companies, but this doesn't mean that it is incapable of growing its earnings.

The economics of its industry look good. Additionally, the political importance of the company in terms of information flow, Baidu is well set for the future.

ZUORA

Market cap - $1.09 billion

52 week high/low - 23.04/6.21

Zuora (pronounced zoo-aura) is yet another stock that has taken a pounding over the past year. On the surface, all news surrounding this company is bad. It hasn't been able to turn a profit as yet, despite going public in 2018 and being founded back in 2007. Its business is in the B2B space which means that a lot of information surrounding it is loaded with technical jargon that is all but incomprehensible to the average investor.

The company was initially founded by two engineers K.V Rao and Cheng Zhou, who worked at WebEx at the time. Rao is the one who had the idea to build a platform that could handle SaaS billing models. These days, the SaaS billing system is everywhere, and from a consumer's perspective, it's pretty easy to handle.

You simply click a button that says subscribe and pay a monthly fee for the software service. However, from a technical standpoint, SaaS is a headache of gargantuan proportions. In 2007, most companies relied on billing their customers once for the product and delivering it. SaaS posed technical challenges to the very architecture of their databases.

Think of it like this: You've built a large mansion only to find that instead of building a single large house, there is greater demand for a number of smaller apartments. You can either tear down the mansion or modify the place to create some sort of a complex, but this isn't going to really do the trick.

Even if you do tear down the place and look to build smaller apartments on the land, who's going to design it for you? Remember that in this analogy, no one has ever built apartments (SaaS databases) before. Therefore, companies were forced to modify their existing databases, and this led to a number of things breaking.

This is what prompted Rao to brainstorm a solution along with Zhou, and they arrived at an initial solution. However, they lacked marketing skills and, as a result, could not convince venture capitalists to back them. This is where the current CEO Tien Tzuo came into the picture.

Tzuo was a big believer in the efficacy of subscription-based models, and as a senior executive at Salesforce, he was well aware of the challenges. Tzuo polished the original ideas and his contacts in the industry managed to land the funding needed, and thus Zuora was born.

While the original founders have since exited amicably, Tzuo continues to function as the chairman and CEO. He's seen as an evangelist for the subscription business model, and has even written a bestselling book on the topic. Zuora currently develops and manages custom solutions to handle subscription payments for their clients.

The problem is that, much like with the evangelist of electric cars, Tzuo's company doesn't make any money. Over the past year, Zuora's stock has dropped by 51%, which is a pretty epic fall for a company so many people expected great things from. So, what's really happening here, and why is Zuora still a great investment?

Business Economics

There's no denying that the subscription-based payment model is here to stay. Zuora happens to be suffering from the pioneer syndrome we previously mentioned. Being the first to the space, the company has had to deal with problems and unforeseeable circumstances every step of the way.

The fact that company revenues have grown every year despite these challenges is a testament to Tzuo's leadership and the ability of senior management to handle tough times. Zuora is a tough company to analyze because it's still effectively in a startup stage despite being a public company. Typically, companies with Zuora's financials don't go public but the lengthy bull market meant the Zuora went public a bit ahead of the curve.

This means that the best way to look at the financial of the company is by looking at its revenue and user growth. Profits might not be present right now, but with continued growth, Zuora stands to capture a significant portion of the market.

The simple reason for such optimism is that there is no other company of its size that poses a threat. Zuora moved first and moved fast in this space, and this gives it a clear head start in terms of technology as well as know-how. Low employee turnover has also meant that the company has done a good job of retaining its knowledge.

This experience is reflected in the diversity of its product lines. The original product that Zuora developed was Zuora billing. This is a turnkey solution for companies and large enterprises to easily migrate their existing one-time payment systems to a subscription-based model.

The other product Zuora integrates with its primary platform is Zuora RevPro which handles all of the accounting needs for subscription-based businesses. Accounting poses a particular headache when it comes to SaaS since GAAP rules specify certain methods in which regular payments need to be booked. It isn't as simple as recording the monthly payments that flow in. GAAP refers to Generally Accepted Accounting Principles that all American firms follow. These are guidelines that define how cash flow is meant to be accounted for on a company's books.

The appeal of RevPro goes beyond just tech-based enterprises. With the way payment methods are changing, the model is extending to pretty much every industry out there. A good example of this is Dollar Shave Club, which operates this model when it comes to men's shaving products.

Some of Zuora's other customers include Harley Davidson and Caterpillar. The revenue model is also quite straightforward. Zuora charges a flat fee plus a monthly volume-based fee. The fees are quite cheap and are far more economical for companies to adopt as opposed to designing their own solution.

All of this puts the spotlight squarely back on customer growth. Instead of charging four customers a quarter each to make a dollar, Zuora aims to charge 100 customers 100 pennies to make a dollar. One of the problems with Zuora's stock is that analysts aren't sure how to set expectations, which reveals one of the problems of an emotion-based market.

The company is being valued at its current level because it isn't meeting expectations. These expectations vary wildly, and as a result, the stock witnessed a lot of volatility. Its revenues grew by 15% the previous year, but despite this, the stock tanked 51%. The sole reason is that revenues didn't grow fast enough, not because there's anything wrong with the company.

It's a bit like receiving $100 and complaining that you didn't receive $1,000 when there was no indication that a payment of $1,000 was possible. These emotional corrections will smooth out over time as Zuora continues to grow. Growth is almost guaranteed thanks to the state of the subscription-based billing model. Meaning that Zuora is a solid long term play.

INTUITIVE SURGICAL

Market cap - $57.74 billion

52 week high/low - 619.00/350.00

Intuitive Surgical sits at the intersection of technology and medicine. Specifically, as the company's name suggests, it is focused on the field of robotic surgery. This field is a crowded one, and it is rife with competition despite the highly technical and specialized nature of the product.

The appeal of robotic surgery is easy to understand. A robotic arm cannot tire or make involuntary mistakes. Despite the term robotic in the name of the process, this doesn't mean that a robot is the one performing surgery. Instead, it is guided by a human being at all times. It's just that the process removes the possibility of involuntary human error.

The demand for robotic surgery first came from the military, which needed emergency medical procedures carried out on soldiers wounded in war zones. In such places, flying a specialist surgeon out would have put them at risk, and this is how Intuitive Surgical first began life.

It has been around for over 20 years now and continues to make money from defense contracts. Its patented DaVinci surgical system is one of the best in the industry. Intuitive is one of the pioneers that came through the tough times in this industry. Now that it's emerged as one of the leaders of a maturing space, it finds itself the target of competition.

This comes in the form of medical giants Medtronic and Stryker deciding to expand their robotic surgery business. Along with this, Johnson and Johnson have announced a partnership with Google to develop and run a wide variety of robotic surgery solutions in the market. All of these companies are far bigger, and it remains to be seen how Intuitive copes with this competition.

Despite all of this, the company has a well-established moat. Intuitive has network effects giving it a wide level of acceptance amongst surgeons. The DaVinci system is simple to use, by surgical standards, and its precision level is unmatched. The system made waves when Intuitive advertised it by performing surgery on a grape to demonstrate how precise the technology is.

The industry itself is witnessing huge growth, which explains why the giants of the sphere are looking at moving in. Studies indicate that patients who experienced surgery with the DaVinci system experienced lesser complications than those who opted for conventional methods.

In addition to this, regulatory approval for surgical robotics has been increasing, and unlike other fast-growing industries such as marijuana and sports betting, there are no hurdles in this regard. People will always need surgery, and as time progresses, robotics are certain to be embraced as acceptable solutions for this. This doesn't mean there are a few issues with Intuitive.

Valuation

One of the downsides of being valued as a tech stock is that a large degree of expectations of growth are factored into the price. This has been true of Intuitive during this decade. As their technology grew and as tech gained widespread exposure, the valuation of Intuitive rose in line with that of other tech companies.

This meant that the stock has been overvalued for a while now. It took an almighty tumble at the beginning of the year before bouncing back up. In this, it is hardly unique and many stocks have witnessed similar behavior. This means that for the first time in many years, Intuitive stock is priced according to its proper value.

This represents a great buying opportunity for investors. One of the reasons the stock went as high as it did was due to the fact that the DaVinci system has been increasingly adopted and as of this writing, the firm declared profits of $1.4 billion on $4.5 billion in sales.

This amount is more than enough to cover its entire cost of production and operating costs. For a company of its size, this is a truly remarkable achievement. The good news is that this number is only expected to increase over time. Over the past two years, net income has increased by 105%.

Of course, Intuitive needs to redirect a significant amount of money into research and development, and this will pose challenges. Typically, R&D efforts take time to bear fruit, and a wrong decision here can set the company back.

However, it isn't as if Intuitive is the only company in this field that is running these risks.

All in all, its fortress-like balance sheet and existing moat make it an attractive investment for the long term.

PAYPAL

Market cap - $124.3 billion

52 week high/low - 124.45/82.07

We've mentioned Elon Musk a few times, and we're now going to highlight his earliest success. PayPal was created by combining Musk's venture X.com with co-founders Peter Thiel, Max Levchin and Luke Nosek's company Cofinity. The company X.com was renamed PayPal and went from strength to strength in the late 90s.

Shortly after its IPO, PayPal became a subsidiary of eBay. A remarkable fact about PayPal is that almost every single one of its original employees went on to found or become early investors in pretty much every Silicon Valley heavy-weight we hear about these days. In no particular order, companies such as Tesla, SpaceX, Facebook, Sequoia Capital, Flickr, Digg, LinkedIn, YouTube, Yelp and Reddit all trace their roots back to the original employees of PayPal.

All of this has given PayPal an even bigger reputational moat as the years go by. People want to work for the company thanks to the cult of personality that its founders have developed. The company continues to become even more bureau-cratic in terms of the way it treats its customers and yet, the sheer weight of its brand name makes it pretty much the only payment processor of choice for a large majority of people.

PayPal is one of those rare companies that has had two IPOs. It was first bought by eBay after its first IPO in 2001, and in 2015, once it became clear that PayPal was eclipsing eBay in terms of sales and profits, the parent company decided to spin it off. Since being detached from eBay, the company has seen remarkable growth.

One of the reasons for PayPal's growth and continued success is the smart acquisition strategy that the company has followed over the years. Let's take a deeper look at why PayPal is such a great investment.

Sector Economics

The digital payments space is set to witness an explosion in activity thanks to the growing unpopularity of cash as a mode of payment. With increasing levels of digitization, governments are finding that extending this to cash and banking transactions helps them recover a greater amount of tax revenues that would have been lost otherwise.

The founding of cryptocurrencies is just the beginning. While cryptocurrencies have not been fully accepted and their exchange is still barred or full of hurdles in many places, governments have taken the hint and have effectively tried to turn their own currencies digital.

Scandinavian countries were some of the first to adopt this tactic. These days a cash payment in those countries attracts an additional cash handling charge at checkout counters. The norm is to usually charge a commission on credit card payments, but here it is reversed. Similar practices are followed in the Netherlands and parts of Western Europe.

The nature of the working economy is also playing a part in this. Clients and suppliers now exist across borders more than ever, and using tired old SWIFT or IBAN bank transfers is a thing of the past. These attract higher levels of fees and also require you to input and set up beneficiaries in your own bank's system. Even after all of this, there is the prospect of the money being routed to the incorrect account.

All of these hindrances have left the payments space wide open for digital solutions to rush into. Banks have responded to this threat by doing nothing and have instead leaned back on their primary cash cow of lending to generate profits. This means that the number of restrictions on digital payments grows less day by day, and cash as a means of transaction will soon be a thing of the past.

Moat

PayPal is the founder of digital payments, and as a result, everyone associates the company with this activity. Small businesses prefer to use PayPal since it's an easy way to receive money without involving tedious bank transfers. Retailers, in general, understand that accepting PayPal is better than not accepting it.

The moat surrounding PayPal is so strong that merchants are willing to accept payments on it despite having to pay high fees. There simply is no other solution at the moment. This is especially true when it comes to the online space. Websites that accept money of any kind integrate PayPal into their structure since users find it best to pay this way.

Acquisitions

As we mentioned earlier, the lack of options in the online payment space is partly because of the acquisitions that PayPal has carried out. One of the best acquisitions PayPal has carried out is with Venmo. Venmo dominates the space of peer to peer payments and is preferred far more than bank transfers.

The app currently has over 40 million accounts and, in the fourth quarter of 2019 handled $29 billion worth of transactions, which comfortably puts it in the lead in p2p payments. This also represents a growth of 56% when compared to the previous year.

While Venmo is used primarily for in-country transactions, Xoom is the platform of choice for cross border transactions. The service is used for far more than money transfers and cash pickups. Xoom also allows its users to recharge mobile phones' balances. Xoom is focused on the phone payments space and faces competition in less developed countries, but as of now, it is the dominant player in South and Central America.

PayPal's acquisition of Honey might not have made waves, but it was a shrewd play to capture a part of the bargain shopping space. The app functions as a browser add-on and as the user shops, it automatically generates coupons that can save money. While the app isn't fully monetized as yet, the tough times that lie ahead certainly bode well for the increase of user numbers.

While Honey didn't make headlines, PayPal's acquisition of MercadoLibre most certainly did. Mercado is South America's largest e-commerce website and far outstrips Amazon in that part of the world. Given the steady rise in users as well as increasing preference for online solutions, PayPal's acquisition price of $750 million seems a pittance to pay for the company.

For comparison's sake, the company generated $1.46 billion in revenue in Brazil alone in 2019.

Digital Nature

PayPal is unique in that, unlike its competitors such as Square, it doesn't have or depend on any in-person interaction. Square is focused more on developing point of sale solutions for merchants, but PayPal has famously stayed away from the business choosing instead to focus only on online payments.

Given the virus outbreak that the world has witnessed recently, this seems like a good decision. While PayPal certainly didn't predict the outbreak, it deserves credit for understanding its business strengths and for sticking to it despite seemingly missing out on an important piece of the puzzle.

While this does increase its exposure to the digital space, and therefore increases its risks. The company is the oldest player in the space and has a wealth of experience to deal with any issues. Its presence around the world is also another sign of strength since it is well versed at this point in handling all regulatory hurdles that authorities put in place.

This places a high cost for newcomers to overcome and allows PayPal to effectively function as a monopoly.

Finances

While Visa and MasterCard are not traditional competitors of PayPal, comparing their financials to PayPal is far more instructive. This is because when it comes to online payments, these three are the only options available for the most part. Given PayPal's focus on the online payments space and the credit card companies' domination of in-person payment methods, you'd expect PayPal to suffer in comparison.

However, this isn't true. Visa carries a far greater debt load on its balance sheet with assets just 1.3x debt. PayPal, on the other hand, is far less leveraged with assets at 7.8x debt. This means it is better suited to handle a downturn. The virus has disrupted the majority of credit card payments due to lockdown measures.

However, PayPal remains unaffected throughout all of this, and even if it were affected, it wouldn't need to worry about creditors. It is in a great financial position.

Small Business

PayPal has been expanding into the lending space and has recently received approval to fund SBA loans through its brand PayPal Credit. This is a major step forward for the company and marks the first time a payment processor is effectively functioning as a bank. While it remains to be seen how PayPal handles the vastly different business, investors don't have too much to worry about.

First off, the size of the business is far smaller than the primary business and given its strong balance sheet, PayPal can afford to take a few risks. Given the economic climate that is likely to exist once lockdown measures lift, there will be a huge demand for loans and being a non-traditional lender will give PayPal a boost in terms of demand.

Risk

A potential risk that PayPal faces is from a phenomenon and not a single company. Blockchain technology has been disrupting existing security measures, and the demand for it grows as the days go by. PayPal is behind the curve with regard to this, and it does face significant security challenges.

This is even more relevant if it's going to be providing loans. The risk here is public perception. While the company hasn't faced any major data breaches, its growing size and reliance on seemingly outdated technology might cause an erosion of trust. As it is, PayPal is not well-liked amongst those who depend on it to receive payments from customers.

The lack of choice is what keeps merchants coming back. If consumers start feeling this way, then the company is in for a tough time. These risks are technological ones and given PayPal's expertise in the space; we do trust that the company will handle it well. Its sheer size as well as its longevity, make it even more likely that PayPal will be a great company for many years to come.

INNOVATIVE INDUSTRIAL PROPERTIES

Market cap - $1.24billion

52 week high/low - 139.53/40.21

Marijuana and medical cannabis have made a huge splash in recent years. The legalization of cannabis in select states in the United States and Canada has opened an entire market for investors to benefit from. The first instinct of many people was to invest in cannabis growers.

Initially, the returns were fantastic. Cannabis stocks rose exponentially for a period of two years but the party ended last year. These stocks fell to such an extent that almost all of them are back to their IPO levels. All in all, while the industry itself has been growing, increasing competition and a strangely efficient black market have ensured that individual companies are facing stiff headwinds.

All of this sounds quite familiar to business historians. We've already mentioned how savvy investors got rich during the gold rush. The same 2nd order consequences principle applies here as well. While everyone is scrambling in a mad dash to grow marijuana and sell them to a public that has been demanding it for years, savvy investors recognize the things that all of these companies need.

There really are two needs when speaking of growing marijuana: Fertilizer and land. As far as fertilizer goes, it isn't as if the plant needs anything special, so there's not much of a moat to be found there. This leaves land, and this is what brings us to marijuana REITs. We've mentioned REITs before when speaking of Crown Castle and how these companies are obligated to pay out 90% of their net cash earnings to their investors.

Innovative Industrial Properties (Innovative) has what is probably the most boring name a company can have, but don't let that put you off. It has a simple business model and utilizes its industry advantages well. It leases land to marijuana growers and earns the rent paid on it. The best part is that the high demand for land to grow marijuana on means that the lease payments are much higher than what you would find when leasing farmland or office space.

This is reflected in the high dividend yield that the company offers its investors. As of current writing, this is at 5.8%, which is almost double that of what a diversified REIT would pay. A diversified REIT invests in a portfolio of properties across functions such as rental real estate, commercial real estate, farmland, hospitals. In short, marijuana suited land is fetching almost double the yield of regular real estate. This is truly a spectacular return.

Lease Structures

One of the advantages that strict legislation in marijuana provides is that lease agreements can be changed from what their terms usually are. This means that all of the properties Innovative provides for lease requires the tenant to pay not just the rent but also the property taxes and maintenance. In industry parlance, such leases are referred to as triple net leases.

This leads to Innovative earning an average cap rate of 13% on its properties. Cap rate refers to the cash return REITs make after all expenses are accounted for. For comparison's sake, the average cap rate of a commercial REIT that leases office buildings is 4%.

This allows Innovative to pay off its mortgage within a seven-year period and after that everything is a profit. We must mention that cap rates are this high right now due to the lack of federal legality. This allows Innovative to charge higher than normal market rates for its properties.

We expect that cap rates will return to normal once legality kicks in across the board. For now, though, rates remain high. The structure of the lease also allows Innovative to incur reduced costs on its properties. Typically, REIT companies have to carry out maintenance and upkeep of their properties.

In Innovative's case, their triple net leases mean that costs are low. While this lowers rental payment as well, it isn't as if it sinks to below market price levels.

Risks

Given that the marijuana industry, at least the legal one, is still immature, there are significant risks the company faces. While it has isolated itself from the majority of fluctuations in the business by becoming a supplier, there are risks nonetheless. Strangely enough, legislation is what provides a threat.

Federal legislation will see rents dropping and leases returning to regular terms, and this will reduce the income that Innovative earns. Growth is what will offset this drop, and in this regard, the company has been doing a great job. It owns over 3.8 million acres of rentable property across the United States and given the high cash on cash return the company earns; expansion is not going to be a problem.

As of now, the company not only pays a high dividend but also pays it quarterly. We expect this amount to decrease a bit as time goes on. These are regular risks that all REITs are exposed to. As long as Innovative sticks to its expertise in the marijuana field and resists the temptation to move into something else, its prospects remain great, and it is a great way to get exposure to the marijuana industry, without the risks of directly investing in growers.

SKYWORKS SOLUTIONS

Market cap - $15.34 billion

52 week high/low - 128.48/66.29

This is yet another stock that is going to feel the boost that 5G will bring this year. 5G is one of the most anticipated technological advances the markets have witnessed in a long time, and that's saying a lot. The technology will provide up to 100 times the speeds of current 4G/LTE networks.

Such speeds are necessary for the development of the internet of things related devices such as smart appliances and driverless cars. Skyworks is a company that manufactures RC chips for smartphone manufacturers and home automation manufacturers. In other words, the semiconductor chips that are a part of every 5G electronic device will likely come from Skyworks.

Currently, 5G phones are expected to comprise 12% of the smartphone market, with the number doubling in 2021 as the technology catches on. This means that the best days for Skyworks are yet to come. Currently, it is a supplier to Apple and Huawei, and if you've been paying attention to the 5G political picture thus far, you'll notice that this is a problem.

The trade war with China and the banning of Huawei from doing business with all American entities has meant that Skyworks has seen its revenues take a hit. This has led to its stock tumbling as the current administration's trade war continues to twist and turn without an end in sight.

However, this isn't bad news for Skyworks as far as the long term is concerned. The technology itself isn't going anywhere, and the company remains the leader in its space. It is more likely than not that increasing demand from consumers will lead to more customers for Skyworks and the reliance on Huawei will be a thing of the past.

To offset this loss, the company has begun including smartphone makers Oppo, Vivo and Xiaomi to increase revenues. Its largest customer remains Apple, and this is a double-edged sword. First off, no company wins the business of Apple unless it happens to have exceptional quality, and Skyworks has been the preferred supplier for many years now.

However, its fortunes are joined at the hip with Apple's, and if the latter faces any challenges with its business, then Skyworks will likely sink with it. Given Apple's size, this is an unlikely event but it remains a risk nonetheless.

Valuation

The best part of Skyworks is that the company is in an extremely sound financial position when compared to its other 5G peers. It has virtually zero debt on its balance sheet, and this puts it in prime position to expand and take more risks should the need arise.

It isn't just the past year but in fact, the last five years that have witnessed debt-free growth. The current pandemic has forced some of its competitors to cut back but Skyworks is now free to expand and conduct business as it pleases. The stock has suffered due to overvaluation that all 5G stocks were subject to.

As we mentioned earlier, a lot of 5G stocks were selling at inflated prices, and once the bubble burst earlier this year, all of these stocks came tumbling down. Skyworks is no different. It got caught up in the general hysteria surrounding the sector and is now selling at a very attractive earnings multiple of 19x.

The main strength of Skyworks is its management without a doubt. They are honest to a point and are incredibly frank when discussing the company's shortcomings on earnings calls.

However, this only reaffirms that the management knows what it's doing, and being conservative in what is an extremely popular sector is good for the long run. All of these will stand Skyworks in good stead, and investors will benefit from this.

Skyworks meets all of our investment criteria, and by reviewing all of them, you'll understand why we highly recommend Skyworks as a long term investment.

This brings to an end our look at the 20 best stocks for you to hold for the next 20 years. All of these companies are wonderful investments, and you'll do well to buy into them at fair prices. Speaking of fair prices, let's move on to an important section of this book - How to value a business.

7

COMPANY VALUATION 101

I t's all well and good choosing a great company to invest in, but if you pay too much, then your returns are greatly impacted.

For example, if you buy Disney at $100/share, when the price hits $150, your return will be 50%. However, if you buy at $125/share, when the price hits $150, your return will only be 20%.

Which leads us to the million dollar question: What is a fair price to pay for a company? There are hundreds of different methods of valuing companies, but we like to keep things simple. You shouldn't need to spend hundreds of dollars on advanced stock screening services, when the most important numbers are available for free on websites like Yahoo Finance or MSN Money.

Here are the numbers we take into account when valuing a business, with a brief definition for each one. We use these after we've done our research on a company and decide that it is worth investing in.

This is so we can determine what is a fair price to pay for 1 share of the business today.

Earnings Per Share (EPS): A company's net income divided by the number of shares available. The higher the better.

Price to Earnings (PE) Ratio: A company's current stock price divided by its Earnings Per Share. The lower the better.

10 Year Equity Growth Rate: This is a calculation popularized by investor and author Phil Town. It refers to the EPS multiplied by the projected growth rate of the company.

Minimum Acceptable Rate of Return: This is the annual growth in a stock you would be happy with. For this, we like to choose a 12% return. We settled on 12% as we want greater returns than the market rate (An average of 9.69% over 50 years). If we were satisfied with market average returns, then we would just buy index funds instead of individual companies. We don't go higher than 12% because we need to take the next metric into account. If you are aiming for higher returns, we also recommend using a higher margin of safety.

Margin of Safety: This refers to a share price being below a businesses' intrinsic value. We want prices to be below intrinsic value to minimize our risk. This is in case our estimates were either incorrect or biased. Margin of Safety also accounts for our "weathering the storm" criteria in chapter 4. If you are aiming for higher annual returns, we also recommend using a higher margin of safety.

These 5 factors combined give us 2 important numbers. A 10 year stock price target and a fair number to pay for that same company today.

When we were writing the first (and second, and third, and fourth) draft of this book, this chapter was the most challenging. We found that the biggest problem with investing books is that it's incredibly challenging to give easy to understand valuation examples in book format. Especially inside an eBook with limited screen space. Even if the valuation models are clear at the time, it was tough for readers to use the information to do their own analysis on companies they were researching.

So we found a solution.

To make things easy for you, we've compiled a free company valuation spreadsheet with all the necessary formulas already inserted. So all you have to do is input the corresponding numbers for the company, and the valuation sheet will tell you whether the company is fairly valued, undervalued or overvalued.

You can download your spreadsheet by using the link below. It's completely free; you don't even need to give your email address.

We've also included our free *Company Valuation 101* video course. This will show you how to use the spreadsheet to complement your own research, as well as the free resources we use to find the 5 important company metrics we discussed earlier in this chapter.

Inside the course we also show you examples of how we use the sheet to value some of the companies listed in the previous chapter.

To get your spreadsheet and video course go to

https://freemanpublications.com/valuation101

8

THE TWO MOST EFFICIENT STOCK BUYING STRATEGIES

W hen it comes to investing your money in the market, there are two ways you can go about doing so. The first is to invest everything you have all at once, and the other is to divide your initial investment into smaller portions. The former method is referred to as lump-sum investing (LS) and the latter is called dollar-cost averaging (DCA).

We'll say this right off the bat: Lump-sum investing is always better. However, there are many ways in which investors complicate the process and often end up confusing LS for DCA. Let's begin by clearly illustrating how LS and DCA work.

LUMP SUM OR DOLLAR COST AVERAGING?

Let's say you have $10,000 to invest. Should you invest all of it at once or should you break it up into smaller investments of $1,000 each and invest these over a period of 10 months? The former method is LS and the latter is DCA.

DCA is not the following: Let's say you receive a steady cash flow of $1,000 per month through your savings after paying for your living expenses. You then invest $1,000 into the market every month like clockwork. This is not DCA. In fact, this is LS investing. We wish to highlight this because many people confuse this for being DCA.

The primary difference between LS and DCA is that with the latter, you're not fully invested in the market. You're setting aside some money as cash at all times. The reasoning behind doing this is that by breaking your investment into smaller parts, you're reducing your risk over a longer period.

For example, if the market declines between months two and six in our previous example, your $1,000 investments over this time will result in you buying stocks at lower prices. This, in turn, reduces your average purchase price, and therefore, you increase the potential size of your capital gains whenever the stock moves upwards.

This works in theory, but it ignores two practical aspects of investing. First, it assumes that the investor practicing the LS method will never invest their money back into the market ever again. Second, it assumes that markets will fall over the short term and that the investor can accurately predict how long they'll fall for.

In other words: If you invest your $10,000 all at once. This is hardly going to be your only stock investment over your lifetime. Who's to say that when you decide to enter the market once again, the market prices will not be low? There's no way to predict this. The DCA reasoning assumes that by investing small amounts over time, you'll reduce your risk.

But what is the appropriate timeline for you to divide your investments into? Should you invest $10,000 over a year? Two years? A decade? This is again, impossible to predict. However, all of this pales in comparison to the real disadvantage of DCA, which is opportunity cost.

Missing Out on Gains

Let's say you invest $10,000 fully into the market. We've already established that the stock market rises by an average of seven percent over the long term. Let's also assume that your investment horizon is 20 years. At the end of this time, your investment will have grown to $38,696.

Now, let's say you practice extreme DCA and divide your $10,000 investment into equal sums and invest it every year for 20 years. This means you'll invest $500 every year. We don't need to run the numbers to prove that this is a losing strategy. With lesser money invested, you're going to be losing out on long term appreciation of capital as well as becoming a victim to inflation. This is where DCA falls horribly short.

You might argue that we're using the assumed return rate of 7% and aren't taking into consideration the fact that the average purchase price might decrease thanks to market declines during this 20 year period. A study that compared the two investing methods using market data from 1960 until 2019 indicates that DCA underperforms lump-sum investing 80% of the time over this period (Maggiulli, 2020).

We must note that DCA outperforms LS during market slumps, as you might expect. However, once the market recovers, LS begins outperforming DCA dramatically and the deficit in performance is erased quickly.

All of this means that instead of asking yourself which method is better when it comes to investing. Focus on having as much of your money invested for as long as possible. This is how returns are earned. This is how you can access greater compounding power. As you know, compounding becomes more powerful the longer you apply it.

Therefore, if you have a large sum of money to invest right now, invest all of it in fairly valued companies. We must emphasize that this doesn't mean putting everything into a single company. You must diversify your investments and use ETFs or mutual funds if necessary. Focus on investing whatever you can, whenever you can. If you have a steady cash flow that allows you to invest money in the market at regular intervals, then do so. Leaving your money sitting on the sidelines doing nothing is the worst possible thing you can do with it.

DRIP

DRIP stands for dividend reinvestment plan. This is a great way to automate your investing and use the power of dividends to boost your returns. They're available on pretty much every dividend paying single, and you're better off opting for them most of the time.

Here's how a DRIP works: When you receive a dividend payment, you can choose to receive it in cash or reinvest that money to buy even more of the stock via a DRIP. By choosing the DRIP option, your broker automatically buys the equivalent amount of shares of stock, and your stock holding increases.

This, in turn, will increase the amount of dividends you'll earn the next time and by reinvesting that sum, you'll increase your stock holding, and this will further increase your dividend and so on.

For example, let's say you own a single share of a stock for $100. This stock pays you a dividend of $2 and you choose the DRIP option. Your broker will buy a fraction of share that is worth $2. Your total number of shares will increase to 1.02 after this. Fractional shares can be bought only via DRIPs. If you receive the dividend as cash and then try to purchase $2 worth of a $100 stock, you won't be able to buy it.

Now that the size of your holding is 1.02 shares, your dividend payment will be slightly greater than before. Assuming the stock still pays $2 per share in dividends, you'll now receive $2.04. If you reinvest this, you'll now own 1.04 shares (up from 1.02). Thus, your dividend payment–as well as your stock holding–increased in number.

The best part about a DRIP is that there are no costs associated with buying these fractional shares. Thus, you get more bang for your buck. Reducing costs has a dramatic effect on overall returns, thanks to compounding. By not paying costs, you'll allow more of your money to compound and are thus capturing greater growth.

The other great aspect of DRIPs is that some companies offer discounts on purchase prices if you choose to invest via a DRIP. Often you can expect a discount of up to 10%. Over time, this will massively boost your capital gains as well as your dividend payment amounts since you'll be able to buy more shares.

In our previous example, additional shares of 0.02 might seem paltry but understand that this assumes prices remain stable. If stock prices decrease, you'll be buying even more shares. When the upswing happens, your gains will proportionally increase. Also, DRIPs work best over time, and this is perfectly in line with the investment principles we outlined previously.

There are a couple of disadvantages you must be aware of when it comes to DRIPs. The first one is that you're not going to be in total control of your money. As long as you've chosen to opt for the DRIP, you're not going to receive the cash into your account. It'll be reinvested all by itself, and this will make some people uncomfortable. If you want to implement a set and forget investment strategy, though, this is the best option for you to choose.

The biggest disadvantage has to do with taxes, but even this isn't as bad as it sounds. Since you won't be receiving money into your account, you might be tempted to think that you don't owe any taxes. However, you will still have to pay taxes on your dividend amounts, and being unaware of this can lead to some nasty surprises during tax time.

Just remember that even if you reinvest the entire sum automatically, you're still liable to pay taxes on your dividend income.

9

MUTUAL FUNDS VERSUS ETFS VERSUS INDIVIDUAL STOCKS

W e've only spoken about individual stocks up to this point, but there are other investing options as well. When it comes to choosing which market instruments you want to invest in, you'll typically end up choosing one of these three. There are some differences between them, and you need to learn these in order to make the best choice. Your choice of instrument comes down to your risk outlook as well as your comfort level with respect to backing your stock picks.

Let's begin by looking at what mutual funds are and how they work.

MUTUAL FUNDS

Mutual funds are one of the oldest investment vehicles that have been in the market. These are issued by financial corporations. Here's how they work: The corporation creates a fund with a certain investment mandate. This could be anything from capturing dividends in small-cap stocks to buying the largest stocks in a certain country, or to create a well-diversified portfolio that invests in everything.

A single unit in the fund is effectively what a share is when speaking of a stock purchase. The fund invests the money it has into stocks of various companies, and all of these underlying stocks have a certain value. When we add these individual values together, we arrive at the total asset value of the fund.

Dividing the total asset value by the number of units gives us the unit price or NAV. The NAV is repriced at the end of every day. This is because the asset value changes depending on the share prices of the underlying stocks.

For example, if mutual fund A owns one share of stock X and one share of stock Y, both of which are priced at $1 each, the NAV is $2. If the prices of X and Y rise to $2, the NAV is now $4.

Since prices keep fluctuating throughout the day, there's no point in calculating the NAV in real time. This is why it is done at the end of the day. During market hours, you can buy mutual fund units, but you'll be purchasing them at the previous day's NAV. There are a few things you must keep in mind when purchasing mutual fund units.

Their objective is to beat the market, and thus, the manager will charge fees that are higher than the other options listed in this chapter. On average, you can expect to pay between 0.5-2% of gains as fees. In addition to this, there are so-called "loading fees."

A front-loading fee is one that is charged when you buy units. The fund manager will deduct a certain amount from your principal, and this will reduce your potential gains. A back-loading fee is charged when you redeem or sell your units. Some funds charge constant load fees, which is to say that they charge maintenance fees during the lifetime of your investment.

Keep in mind that a mutual fund can either charge all of these fees or some combination of them. Due to investors' increased sensitivity to fees, some mutual funds offer no-load features and have you pay just the fee on whatever gains you make. Typically, no-load funds have higher performance fees.

The best way to get a handle on performance fees is to look at the expense ratio. This number is calculated by dividing the total cost of running the fund by the total assets. Keep in mind that expense ratios don't always include loading fees.

One advantage of mutual funds is that if you choose to buy an in house fund from your broker (a fund that is run by the brokerage itself) you'll likely pay zero commissions on it. This will reduce your investment costs in the long run. Mutual funds don't make the most sense these days as an investment.

Despite certain advantages, this is primarily due to the presence of the next option we'll discuss. However, there are a few exceptional ones you can invest in. It's just that finding them is tough.

EXCHANGE-TRADED FUNDS

ETFs were born from a need to reduce investment expenses. Mutual fund loading fees tend to reduce gains quite a bit. ETFs trade just like regular stocks do in the market. In other words, unlike with mutual funds, you'll see their prices fluctuate up and down intraday.

In terms of structure, ETFs are built just like mutual funds are. They're issued by large corporations and can have a number of investment objectives. In fact, compared to mutual funds, ETFs have a larger number of objectives.

For example, you can buy so-called inverse ETFs. These ETFs increase in price as market prices decline. You can buy an inverse ETF for a particular sector or the entire market. Then there are leveraged ETFs that move in a given direction faster than their underlying stocks. For example, if you buy a 2X leveraged broad market ETF, the ETF will rise at twice speed of the underlying market. On the other hand, it will fall just as fast, so it's not as if these aren't without risk.

You will also find inverse leveraged ETFs, so as you can see, it's possible to get quite complicated with these things. With that being said, you can invest in ETFs that aim to simply capture the average return of an index or a group of stocks. For example, you can buy an ETF that aims to capture the performance of a group of dividend-paying stocks.

ETFs have expense ratios as well, but the ones that aim to capture average market performance have lower expense ratios. These typically are under 1%, so they're a lot cheaper to maintain than mutual funds, and this boosts your gains over the long term. When it comes to ETFs it's best to keep it simple and not opt for ones that have obscure investment strategies.

This is because many ETFs are created by investment banks to find people to take the other side of trades that hedge funds wish to take (Blitz, 2017). For example, if a hedge fund approaches their investment bank (their brokers) and wishes to create a portfolio that they wish to short (profit when the prices decrease). They need to borrow money from the bank to invest in this portfolio. The bank then has to find someone else to take the other side of this trade. If they fail to find any institutional investors to take this bet, they often end up creating an ETF that contains the same underlying stocks and is leveraged. Thus, you might end up buying this leveraged, long ETF while the hedge fund is on the other side of your trade. As prices decrease, you're unlikely to be able to exit this investment since they're not going to be heavily marketed, and thus, fewer people will be trading them.

You can buy ETFs that mimic hedge fund strategies, but you must conduct thorough research to see if these strategies are based on sound investment principles.

FREEMAN INVESTING RULE #11

NOT ALL ETFs ARE CREATED EQUAL. ENSURE YOU KNOW HOW THE FUND OPERATES BEFORE YOU INVEST IN ONE.

Taxes

One advantage of ETFs is that their tax profile is a bit easier to handle than that of mutual funds. Mutual funds often return capital gains as distributions to their investors. Thus, you'll find yourself paying capital gains on your dividends from the fund, even if you haven't sold a single unit. This does complicate the calculation of your taxes when the time comes.

In contrast, ETFs don't distribute capital gains back to their investors. You'll pay capital gains only when you sell your investment for a profit. The interim distributions are taxed as dividends are. For example, if your dividend distribution contains a portion of international stock dividends, domestic dividends, and REIT payments, your 1099-DIV from your broker will break all of this down clearly, and you'll pay taxes on these portions as per IRS rules.

As with mutual funds, you don't have control over the way your money is invested. The fund manager is the one that decides where your money goes. Your comfort level with this depends on the kind of approach you're taking in the market. This is a good time to highlight the differences between passive and active investing.

PASSIVE VERSUS ACTIVE

Passive investing refers to when an investor simply sits back and aims to capture the average performance of the market. In other words, you invest in an ETF that tracks the S&P 500 index, and your investment is tied to its performance. This way, you can capture the broad market performance over the long run. Since the market will increase in size over this time, you're guaranteed to capture these gains.

Your downside risk is also significantly limited since the ETF is diversified. After all, it holds shares in every company that is a part of the index. While a single stock might decrease in value, it's unlikely that every single stock is going to fall all at once over the long term.

The flip side is that you're going to earn whatever the market earns and will not outperform it. However, do keep in mind that this brings ample peace of mind. Contrast this with active investing where you're concentrating your investment into a few stocks with the aim of capturing huge capital gains.

While your potential gains are high, so is your downside risk. As we explained in Chapter 5, with a highly concentrated portfolio, there is a greater risk that all of your investments could decline in value. You'll also need to remain on top of the news surrounding the stock. All in all, both options have their pros and cons, and it comes down to what sort of risk you're willing to undertake.

If you feel that you cannot stomach the thought of long term losses, then you're probably better off following a fully passive model. For most investors, though, a hybrid model works best. This is what we've suggested in this book. You'll be investing in common stocks that have been identified using sound principles for the long term.

By investing in individual stocks, you won't be paying any management fees either. After all, you're investing in them by yourself, so why would you need to pay anyone? If your broker charges commissions, you'll be paying this amount, of course. Best of all, you won't be losing the opportunity to buy an undervalued stock like you would if you invest in an ETF.

"A LOT OF PEOPLE WITH HIGH IQS ARE TERRIBLE INVESTORS BECAUSE THEY'VE GOT TERRIBLE TEMPERAMENTS. AND THAT IS WHY WE SAY THAT HAVING A CERTAIN KIND OF TEMPERAMENT IS MORE IMPORTANT THAN BRAINS. YOU NEED TO KEEP RAW IRRATIONAL EMOTION UNDER CONTROL. YOU NEED PATIENCE AND DISCIPLINE AND AN ABILITY TO TAKE LOSSES AND ADVERSITY WITHOUT GOING CRAZY. YOU NEED AN ABILITY TO NOT BE DRIVEN CRAZY BY EXTREME SUCCESS."

- Charlie Munger

10

THE MOST IMPORTANT INGREDIENT OF SUCCESSFUL INVESTING

W hat is the key to your long term investment success? It all comes down to your ability to hold onto your investment even when the market declines. This is arguably the most important principle of successful investing, and many inexperienced investors fail this test because of the way they think about the markets.

THE DIFFERENCE BETWEEN REALIZED AND UNREALIZED RETURNS

A common mistake people make when thinking about their stock investments is that they confuse unrealized gains for realized ones. Realized gains or losses refer to the cash return or loss you incur on your investments. If you bought something for $10 and sold it for $15, you've earned a realized gain of $5.

However, if you've bought something for $10 and its price is now sitting at $7, you have an unrealized loss of $3. In other words, you haven't lost any money as yet. The problem is that most people see the red $3 in their investment accounts and think that they're $3 poorer and hurry to sell in case they 'lose' even more.

FREEMAN INVESTING RULE #12

NO GAINS OR LOSSES ARE REAL
UNTIL YOU SELL

People sell for all kinds of reasons, most of them emotional ones. You might switch to your favorite financial channel and see that everything is falling and that 'investors have lost $1 trillion in value' or some such nonsensical headline. These numbers are a picture of the unrealized losses in the market. You will realize them only by selling your investment.

Over the short term, emotions are what drive market prices. The father of value investing, Benjamin Graham coined a term to describe this phenomenon. He created a persona called Mr. Market to represent how the market behaves. Mr. Market is an extremely irrational person, and every day, he comes up to you and offers you prices for his products.

One day he might come to you and tell you that Coca-Cola stock is worth $2,000. The next day, he'll be supremely dejected for some reason and will offer to sell you Coca-Cola for $80. The notion that a giant of a company such as Coca-Cola can have such huge fluctuations in value over a single day makes no sense to him. He listens to his emotions, and that's it.

Many people get carried away by the turmoil that Mr. Market experiences. They believe his words when he tells them that everything is going to fall apart. They believe him when he tells them that COVID-19 is going to result in Chinese hegemony over the U.S for the foreseeable future and that 5G marks the complete destruction of all American enterprise and so on.

They listen to these notions and invest in unknown Chinese stocks and then wonder why they've ended up losing all of their money. We're not saying that Chinese stocks are bad. The point is that following your emotions when investing and not taking a look at the business is a surefire way to lose money.

Law of Averages

The companies mentioned in this book are in a great position to perform well over the next two decades. Will *all* of them fulfill this promise? Probably not. Business is an uncertain thing, to begin with, and no one can ever promise sure-fire returns. However, the objective here is to line up as many factors in our favor as possible and then let the probabilities take over.

One company might not work out. Two might not. But all 20? This is pretty unlikely. The probabilities tell us this. Think of it this way: If you're tossing a coin, you know that you have a 50% chance of calling the result correctly. Does this mean you'll be right every single time if you call heads? Probably not.

However, can you reasonably guess how many times you'll be right over 1,000 coin flips? Yes, you can. You'll be right calling heads roughly 500 times. How about 10,000? In this case, you can be even more certain since the longer you flip the coin, the more you give the probabilities a chance to work out.

It's the same with building a stock portfolio. Invest in sound companies with a long term vision and sit back and let it do its thing.

Emotions are not Facts

On February 19th, Duke played North Carolina in a college basketball matchup that always draws a ton of attention. Duke's star player and future number one NBA draft pick Zion Williamson tried pivoting two minutes into the game and discovered himself on the floor shortly thereafter. It turns out, his Nike shoe had exploded.

By exploded, we mean exploded. It didn't tear or come apart at the seams. One side of his shoe literally burst open, and Williamson was done for the game. The next day, a ton of negative press followed. It turns out that Nike's shoes were making a habit of exploding during critical times.

The press accused Nike of downplaying the incident, and soon, financial news was full of speculation as to whether Nike was now a good short or whether its stock was overvalued. In the hysteria, everyone forgot to ask a simple question: Was this crisis large enough for an entire generation of NBA and sports fans to dump Nike? Would they really dump the brand that owned the Jordan brand of shoes? Can a single exploding shoe really sink a $100 billion-dollar company?

Similar hysteria surrounds Disney at the moment, as we've already outlined. Basing your investment decisions on such short term emotional cues is a surefire way to lose money. Always keep the principles we've outlined in mind before making any decision.

Personal Finances

A good way to minimize your chances of doing something irrational is to avoid any chances of being so. This means you need to have your personal finances in order before investing in the market, as we've already mentioned. If you feel the need to make quick money from the market, you're unlikely to succeed. We refer to our earlier quote about the best way to make $1 million quickly in the stock market. Start with $2 million and go from there.

For example, if you find that you're short of cash to pay your phone bills, you're more likely to sell your investment holdings to raise cash. Eliminating the need for this cash is the best option to pursue. It is best to save at least three months' worth of living expenses along with any emergency cash you might need.

Do not invest money that you might need for the next ten years, at the very least. This way, you'll be able to stay out of your own way and won't sabotage yourself. Do not look at your investments as a savings account that you can tap into in times of need. This will lead you to sell at lows and buy at highs, which is the opposite of what you should do to make money.

Another point to remember is that if your investment principles are sound, and if the original conditions that caused you to invest in the company still exist, then declining stock prices are good news for you. This allows you to get into the stock at discounted prices. Often, investors look at it the other way and see falling market prices as proof that they were wrong.

Use intelligent investment principles, and you'll find that stock market investment will work wonders for you over the long run.

11

WHEN TO SELL

If you've followed the lesson on unrealized and realized gains properly, you'll have understood that selling is what determines your profit or loss. With this in mind, when should you sell? Most investors get the selling aspect of their investment all wrong and end up selling right when they should be buying.

The question of selling can quickly become a complicated one if you take your life events into account. This chapter aims to simplify the question for you, and by the end of it, you'll have a good idea of how you need to approach this question.

REASONS TO SELL

Broadly speaking, there are just three reasons for which you should be selling your stocks:

1. Investment reasons no longer exist
2. Compromised management
3. Better opportunities

Investment Reasons *no Longer Exist*

You've invested in a stock for a particular reason. Let's say you liked its prospects given the upcoming 5G revolution and think that the company is well placed to take advantage of this. You also notice that the stock is selling at a relatively cheap price, given these prospects and buy in wholeheartedly.

Fast forward eight years and you find that the 5G space has become quite crowded and your company hasn't quite kept up with competition as well as you'd hoped. Its products still have some demand, but there are clearly other ones out there that clients prefer with increasing frequency. In short, the reasons that you based your investment on are no longer valid. Such situations indicate that it's best for you to exit your investment and sell it.

Often, you might find that the core business is no longer relevant. For example, Blockbuster was a great company for many years and was well ahead of the curve when it came to in-home DVD rentals. However, they didn't adapt to the streaming revolution. In fact, Blockbuster turned down the chance to buy Netflix on 3 separate occasions.

As a result, they went bankrupt. You didn't have to wait until bankruptcy to figure out that the company had issues. The warning signs were there early on in terms of decreasing earnings as well as increased expenses. Blockbuster was a behemoth that simply couldn't turn around in time.

Borders is another example of this. The firm was extremely slow to react to the threat that Amazon posed. While its main competitor, Barnes & Noble, struggles on thanks to its brand name and a good location strategy, Borders instead shrunk the floor space it dedicated to books. It began incorporating all kinds of products that had nothing to do with books instead and focused on opening smaller outlets.

Perhaps the worst decision of all was to completely eliminate all seating areas that book lovers prefer within book stores. The company reasoned that this would force patrons to buy more stuff. Instead, patrons simply went to Barnes & Noble instead. All in all, the chances of a bookstore surviving while moving away from books is a bit unrealistic. This alone would have sent alarm bells ringing in the mind of any intelligent investor.

Lastly, we have the most famous case of failure to adapt: Kodak. The company famously doubled down on film roll and neglected the realm of digital cameras. As a result, it's nowhere to be found these days.

Compromised Management

At the turn of the millennium, there was one company that dominated the markets to such an extent that these days, it's unthinkable to imagine. Think of the sort of headlines Amazon, Apple and Google generate, and you'll have an idea of what Enron was like. This company was based out of Houston and was an energy trading firm.

Its business area was sufficiently complex enough for outsiders to worship management as being brilliant, and the firm ticked all the boxes with regard to political connections to be intimidating to competitors. For example, George W. Bush and Dick Cheney were close to the company's chairman Kenneth Lay and the chief financial officer Jeff Skilling.

Given all of this, it came as a huge shock that Enron was bankrupt, and even worse, it had been bankrupt for quite a few years running and had been cooking its books in complicity with its auditing firm, Arthur Andersen (now Accenture). The only reason Lay isn't vilified more than he is for his role in the scandal is because of the supervillain like actions that Jeff Skilling carried out.

An example of this was when Skilling dumped all of his stock prior to an earnings release while still exhorting employees to buy more stock in the company. Skilling even went so far as to abuse an analyst who dared question the financial condition of Enron's books during an earnings call.

Dishonest management will always reveal themselves without prompting. Lay and Skilling's behavior was notorious well before the scandal, and Enron's culture was toxic at all times. However, people ignored this since the company made ungodly sums of money.

Another example of this was the former Wall Street giant Lehman Brothers. This was another case where an earnings call with analysts revealed deep flaws in the company's books. In this instance, the CFO of Lehman, Erin Callan was questioned by the hedge fund manager David Einhorn. In Callan's defense, she wasn't committing fraud. Lehman was just too incompetent to figure out the true nature of the assets they were carrying.

The firm went bust during the credit crisis, and Einhorn was one of the first people to warn of the dangers that banks were running, even if he didn't have a movie made around him. The case of Radioshack's CEO falsifying his academic credentials also comes to mind.

Small lies eventually lead to bigger lies. If you begin to spot inconsistencies in the way management communicates its shortcomings or if it begins to treat everyone else like a bunch of dunces, most likely it is the management that is incompetent. You're best served by getting out quickly.

Better Opportunities

Stocks don't always go up. At some point, they will consolidate, and their prices will remain at a certain level for years. This is not a bad thing by itself. If you do happen to find a better company to invest in and if you've earned at least a 50% gain on your investment, then feel free to sell your holdings and move your money to the new venture. Remember that you will need to pay capital gains taxes when you do sell stocks at a profit. Treat the entire sale as if you're selling a house and buying a new one. Carry out the level of preparation that such a transaction demands.

Alternatively, if you made a poor investment decision in the past (we all do), it's ok to take a loss. Remember to analyze why the stock's price is lower than when you bought. If you don't believe anything about the core business has changed, then keep holding. However, if your initial research was off the mark, or the underlying sector economics no longer make sense, then you are free to sell. It's important to analyze your losses and understand why you were wrong in the first place. This will help you make better decisions going forward. Remember you can write off capital losses come tax season.

PUTTING IT ALL TOGETHER

As we come to the end of this book, you now have a significant opportunity on your hands. While the financial media want you to believe that stock investing is a tough art to master, the best way to get ahead is to use the simple and easy to understand principles you've learned in this book. This is because the simpler your principles are, the less likely you are to overcomplicate things.

Remember to keep the investment principles we spoke about earlier in your mind at all times. These alone will ensure an intelligent investment and will significantly reduce your chances of losing money. Here they are again, briefly:

- The Warren Buffett test - Buy great business at fair prices. See if you can describe the business to a 10-year-old.
- Understand the true business - How well do you know what drives the profits of the business?
- Founder syndrome - How honest and reliable is management? Is there a succession plan in place, or does it all depend on the founder?
- Intangible assets - Does the company have any brand loyalty? Does it have intellectual property like patents or trademarks? Things which don't show up on a balance sheet
- Management quality - How well does management align the business with the economics of the industry? How well do they reinvest capital?
- Sales and marketing - How dedicated is the company to sales and marketing? What is the quality of their teams? How are their key metrics looking year-to-year?
- Long term focus - Is management focused on short term metrics, or does it invest resources for the long run?
- Moat - A moat is a phenomenon that gives a company an unfair

advantage in its field. It could be brand loyalty, a superior supply chain, sheer size, etc.

- Can it weather a storm? - How well will the business perform under a stress test?

Ask yourself all of these questions prior to investing in a company. As you can see, they require a high degree of honesty from yourself. It also requires you to stay away from fad and currently popular industries if your sole reason for investment is their popularity. Instead, evaluate the company's fundamental business and management.

Above all else, remember that a share is a slice of the business. You aren't someone only in it for the short run. You're an owner of the company. So, behave like one!

We wish you all the luck and profits in the world and are positive that implementing our Rational Process Investing system will help you earn all the profits you deserve.

One final word from us. If this book has helped you in any way, we'd appreciate it if you left a review on Amazon. Reviews are the lifeblood of our business. We read every single one, and incorporate your feedback into future book projects.

To leave an Amazon review go to https://freemanpublications.com/leaveareview

"THE MOST SUCCESSFUL PEOPLE IN LIFE ARE THE ONES WHO ASK QUESTIONS. THEY'RE ALWAYS LEARNING. THEY'RE ALWAYS GROWING. THEY'RE ALWAYS PUSHING."

- Robert Kiyosaki

CONTINUING YOUR JOURNEY

Like Robert Kiyosaki said on the previous page, the most successful people in life are always learning, growing, and asking questions.

Which is why we created our investing community, so that likeminded individuals could get together to share ideas and learn from each other.

We regularly run giveaways, share wins from our readers, and you'll be the first to know when our new books are released.

It's 100% free, and there are no requirements to join, except for the willingness to learn.

You can join us on Facebook by going to

http://freemanpublications.com/facebook

REFERENCES

Blitz, David, Are Hedge Funds on the Other Side of the Low-Volatility Trade? (January 12, 2017). Available at SSRN: https://ssrn.com/abstract=2898034 or http://dx.doi.org/10.2139/ssrn.2898034

Daszkowski, D. (2019). What's Required to Open a McDonald's Franchise?. Retrieved 16 April 2020, from https://www.thebalancesmb.com/requirements-to-open-a-McDonald's-franchise-1350970

DiLallo, M. (2019). Why Cell Tower REITs Stand Above the Rest. Retrieved 16 April 2020, from https://www.fool.com/millionacres/real-estate-investing/articles/why-cell-tower-reits-stand-above-rest/

Graham, B., & Dodd, D. (1934). Security analysis. New York: McGraw-Hill.

Gupta, R. (2020). How Far Is Netflix From Target Of 100 Million India Subscribers?. Retrieved 16 April 2020, from https://marketrealist.com/2020/02/how-far-netflix-100-million-subscribers-india/

LaRoche, J. (2019). Yahoo is now a part of Verizon Media. Retrieved 16 April 2020, from https://finance.yahoo.com/news/warren-buffett-quotes-from-the-annual-letter-215739887.html

Lee, J., Kim, J. and Bae, J., (2016). Founder CEOs and Innovation: Evidence from S&P 500 Firms. SSRN Electronic Journal

Lewis, M. (2011). The Big Short. New York: W.W. Norton

Lieber, C. (2015). Inside Lululemon's Booming Underground Resale Market. Retrieved 16 April 2020, from https://www.racked.com/2015/3/12/8198483/lululemon-ebay-facebook-resale-secondary-market

Lieber, C. (2018). Lululemon's ex-CEO wrote an outrageous "unauthorized" history of the brand. Here's what we learned. Retrieved 16 April 2020, from https://www.vox.com/the-goods/2018/10/22/18010410/chip-wilson-lululemon-athleisure-book

Maggiulli, N. (2020). Dollar Cost Averaging vs. Lump Sum: The Definitive Guide – Of Dollars And Data. Retrieved 16 April 2020, from https://ofdollarsanddata.com/dollar-cost-averaging-vs-lump-sum/

Martin, E. (2018). Only 23% of millennials prefer investing to cash—here's why they're skeptical of the stock market. Retrieved 16 April 2020, from https://www.cnbc.com/2018/08/01/why-millennials-are-scared-of-the-stock-market.html

Mckenna, B. (2020). Yahoo is now a part of Verizon Media. Retrieved 16 April 2020, from https://finance.yahoo.com/news/3-key-ceo-quotes-zoom-144500599.html

Mitchell, C. (2019). The Two Biggest Flash Crashes of 2015. Retrieved 16 April 2020, from https://www.investopedia.com/articles/investing/011116/two-biggest-flash-crashes-2015.asp

O'Kane, S. (2020). Tesla's record 2019 has bought it some breathing room. Retrieved 16 April 2020, from https://www.theverge.com/2020/1/29/21113987/tesla-q4-2019-earnings-results-profit-revenue-model-3

Orem, T. (2020). 2019-2020 Capital Gains Tax Rates & How to Avoid a Big Bill - NerdWallet. Retrieved 16 April 2020, from https://www.nerdwallet.com/blog/taxes/capital-gains-tax-rates/

Rydon, M. (2020). The Upshot. Retrieved 16 April 2020, from https://www.nytimes.com/section/upshot

Saibil, J. (2020). Disney Is Buying More Land. Is a New Theme Park on the Way? | The Motley Fool. Retrieved 16 April 2020, from https://www.fool.com/investing/2020/04/02/disney-is-buying-more-land-is-a-new-theme-park-on.aspx

Schwartz, N. (2000). Inside the Market's Myth Machine In pushing Amazon's stock to irrational heights, Wall Street bulls boosted their own careers. Amazon's doubters--even when they were right--haven't fared nearly as well. - October 2, 2000. Retrieved 16 April 2020, from https://archive.fortune.com/magazines/fortune/fortune_archive/2000/10/02/288462/index.htm

Wagner, K. (2019). Facebook almost missed the mobile revolution. It can't afford to miss the next big thing. Retrieved 16 April 2020, from https://www.vox.com/2019/4/29/18511534/facebook-mobile-phone-f8

What is the difference between 4G and 5G?. (2020). Retrieved 16 April 2020, from https://www.justaskgemalto.com/en/difference-4g-5g

Wolfers, J. (2020). The Unemployment Rate Is Probably Around 13 Percent. Retrieved 16 April 2020, from https://www.nytimes.com/2020/04/03/upshot/coronavirus-jobless-rate-great-depression.html

Yuan, E. (2020). Zoom's Use of Facebook's SDK in iOS Client - Zoom Blog. Retrieved 16 April 2020, from https://blog.zoom.us/wordpress/2020/03/27/zoom-use-of-facebook-sdk-in-ios-client/

Zafar, Z. (2020). The Trade Desk: Time Is Running Out For Linear TV. Retrieved 16 April 2020, from https://seekingalpha.com/article/4337232-trade-desk-time-is-running-out-for-linear-tv

Made in the USA
Monee, IL
05 December 2021

83982966R00114